CONCEPTIONS OF
Islamic Education

A.C. (Tina) Besley, Michael A. Peters,
Cameron McCarthy, Fazal Rizvi
General Editors

Vol. 3

The Global Studies in Education series is part of the Peter Lang Education list.
Every volume is peer reviewed and meets
the highest quality standards for content and production.

PETER LANG
New York • Washington, D.C./Baltimore • Bern
Frankfurt • Berlin • Brussels • Vienna • Oxford

Yusef Waghid

CONCEPTIONS OF
Islamic Education

PEDAGOGICAL FRAMINGS

PETER LANG
New York • Washington, D.C./Baltimore • Bern
Frankfurt • Berlin • Brussels • Vienna • Oxford

Library of Congress Cataloging-in-Publication Data

Waghid, Yusef.
Conceptions of Islamic education: pedagogical framings / Yusef Waghid.
p. cm. — (Global studies in education; v. 3)
Includes bibliographical references.
1. Islamic education. I. Title.
LC903.W36 371.828'297—dc22 2011012666
ISBN 978-1-4331-1204-1 (hardcover)
ISBN 978-1-4331-1203-4 (paperback)
ISSN 2153-330X

Bibliographic information published by **Die Deutsche Nationalbibliothek**.
Die Deutsche Nationalbibliothek lists this publication in the "Deutsche
Nationalbibliografie"; detailed bibliographic data is available
on the Internet at http://dnb.d-nb.de/.

The paper in this book meets the guidelines for permanence and durability
of the Committee on Production Guidelines for Book Longevity
of the Council of Library Resources.

© 2011 Peter Lang Publishing, Inc., New York
29 Broadway, 18th floor, New York, NY 10006
www.peterlang.com

Printed in the United States of America

Contents

Preface

The 9/11 attacks on the Twin Towers in the United States altered the common perceptions about Muslims. Despite all the questions asked and justifications offered, there has been a deluge of accusations against Muslims. Even more so, Muslims responsible for these acts of terror have been branded as conservative, fundamentalist and mostly trained in the radical *madrassahs* (*madāris*) which tarnished the image of liberal, moderate Islam. Thus, Muslims and Islamic education have been under scrutiny from all ends of the globe. People want answers as to why some people could perpetrate acts of violence against others in the name of Islam. Invariably, in some instances Islamic educational institutions are blamed for initiating some people into discourses of terror, whereas in other instances Islamic education is considered to be a dogmatic practice that instigates some people to take extremist actions against others.

My motivation to write this book was spawned both by my earlier work on Islamic education in the 1990s in South Africa, and by my ongoing intellectual engagement with issues of democratic citizenship, cosmopolitanism and pedagogy. After I presented the paper 'Islamic education in South Africa: Contesting the boundaries of extremism' at the Institute of the Malay World and Civilization, Universiti Kebangsan Malaysia on 16 September 2009, I became more interested in completing this project. I subsequently visited Malaysia again in September 2010 to continue working on this book and received unselfish encouragement from my colleague and friend, Professor Wan Mohd Nor Wan Daud. As a South African Muslim I have sufficient reason to believe that my ancestors come from the Indonesian Archipelago. Not surprisingly, Wan Mohd Nor who works at the Institute would always tell me that I would be mistaken for a Malay. Muslims who reside in the picturesque Bo-Kaap district of Cape Town at the foot of Table Mountain are often referred to as Cape Malays. Yet, these Muslims (including myself) do not speak the Malay language neither do they in fact have a language of their own other than a strange combination of Afrikaans (commonly known as the language of the coloniser and later apartheid oppressor), English, Malay and Arabic. These languages combined are commonly known as *kombuis* (kitchen) Afrikaans, or a colloquial type of Afrikaans. In many ways then, this book reflects my personal connection with Islam in Southeast Asia, considering that in the 17th century Islam became established in South Africa with the arrival of slaves, political exiles and indentured workers from the Indonesian Archipelago and the South Asian subcontinent. Ibrahim of Batavia was the first Muslim who arrived at the Cape with Jan van Riebeeck on 6 April 1652. Shaykh Yusuf of Macassar arrived in 1694 as a political exile and formed the first Muslim community on a farm at Zandvliet. Rajah of Tambora (Java), who arrived in 1697, wrote down the first Qurān in the Cape from memory; he later handed this copy to Simon van der Stel, the Governor of the Cape (after whom the town of Stellenbosch was named— the university where I work is situated here). Tuan Saʿīd arrived in 1744 and was incarcerated on Robben Island for eleven years (the same island from which Nelson Mandela was released after 27 years). Tuan Guru (Imam Abdullah Kadi Abdu al-Salām) arrived on 6 April 1780 and was imprisoned on the same island. Upon his release in 1793 he agitated for the first mosque and led the first congregational prayers in defiance of the law. He also established the first Islamic school in Dorp Street, Bo-Kaap, which was to become the site of the first mosque in Cape Town—*Masjid al-Awwal*. It was from this school that Arabic-Afrikaans emerged. The Afrikaans language is a combination of Dutch, Arabic and Malay, and the first Afrikaans book in Roman script was published in 1862.

Currently, there are about two million Muslims in South Africa, mainly made up of Cape Muslims (mostly in the surroundings of Cape Town), Indian Muslims (mostly in the Gauteng and KwaZulu-Natal provinces), indigenous African Muslims, and other immigrant Muslims from Somalia, Zimbabwe, Malawi, Egypt and other African countries. In the main, Muslims constitute about 2% of the population and there are more than 600 mosques, over 400 Islamic educational institutions, colleges, private schools and tertiary colleges. Of particular interest then to this book, are the *madāris* (afternoon Muslim schools) where I happened to have taught for several years during the 1980s and early 1990s. Most of the ideas I developed in this book have in some way been inspired by my involvement as both Muslim teacher in a *madrassah* for almost two decades as well as a brief stint as religious leader of a mosque congregation in the early 1990s whilst pursuing my doctoral studies in philosophy of Islamic education. The main thrust of this book is to argue that *madāris* cannot exclusively be held responsible for the cultivation of extremism. Let me introduce my argument as a South African Muslim (having been involved with *madāris* for some part of my life) as follows: The claim is that the first seeds of extremism were planted by the early Muslims at the Cape and that these extremist ideas must have filtered down to the Muslim schools (*madāris*) today. Of course, there have been several differences amongst Muslims during the early days of colonialism, which resulted in the proliferation of mosques in the Cape Town environs (Davids, 1980). These religious differences did not result in violence. In fact, Tuan Guru's ('Mr Teacher's') defiance of the law when he led the first congregational prayers was a peaceful act of political resistance against the then oppressive colonial regime which denied people the right to freedom of religious expression. The fact that he led a congregational prayer (as an act of peaceful devotion to Allāh Almighty) cannot be construed as an act of violent aggression but rather a bold act in the face of an unjust and insolent government that refused people their right to freedom of religion. Also, the mushrooming of mosques was first and foremost an indication of the expansion of the Islamic faith rather than an act of intolerance towards one another. If this were to have been the case, Muslim schools (which actually collaborate on many fronts) would have existed in stark opposition to each other. I have no reason to believe that this is the case and I have never encountered any Muslim learner at a *madrassah* who blatantly wanted to overthrow the state as an act of violence. Considering South Africa's history of racial segregation and oppression and the fact that almost two decades after the first democratic government took over, all people (including Muslims) now have the franchise denied them in the past, this would not make any sense.[1] Once again my potential critic might argue that the People Against Gangsterism and Drugs (PAGAD) movement (a community organisation) comprised mostly of Muslims is violent particularly because of their allegedly over-extended aggressive tactics used against drug lords and the lynching of one gang member who subsequently passed away. The democratic state took strong action against the leadership of this movement and several of its members are currently serving prison sentences for inciting public violence. However, whether one should associate the activities of PAGAD with the educational discourses at Muslim schools is a bridge too far, primarily because the education system in these *madāris* encourages the cultivation of active and non-violent citizenship (as I shall argue for later on in this book).

Also, the education system implemented in public schools in South Africa is an outcomes-based education system devised by the democratic state as part of its symbolic severance from apartheid education which left many learners underprepared for tertiary education. The apartheid state was intent on reserving higher education for the white minority and therefore education in public schools were considered as 'fundamental' to the life world of only the white learner. There have been catastrophic inequities between white education and that experienced by the generically black communities (including coloureds, Indians and African blacks). Since 1994 education has been considered to be democratic, serving the interests of all learners, including those attending Muslim schools. Although the new system of education is not flawless[2] it at least encourages learners to participate as critical and active citizens in a new democracy. So any accusation that Muslim learners (who mostly attend these schools during the day and only attend *madāris* in the afternoon) are taught to be radical in their ways of behaviour and should undermine the democratic secular state for not being Islamic does not hold water at all. Instead, education in public schools is designed to produce a learner who can participate actively in relation to others, as well as to contribute to reconciliation and nation building after decades of disastrous apartheid rule.

In addition to the OBE system of education into which learners are initiated, they are also exposed to Islamic Studies and Arabic where they are often taught by religious leaders, mostly at afternoon *madāris*. Now if the argument were to be used that it is during learners' exposure to pure Islamic discourses that they are indoctrinated to be radical and rebellious, then such a view can easily be dispelled on the grounds that their initiation into revealed Islamic studies is not seen as separate to their learning but rather complementary to their understandings of non-revealed sciences. In a nutshell: learners are taught (through Islamic Studies) to respect one another and to demonstrate compassion for all South Africa's citizens, irrespective of differences in race, colour, ethnicity, culture or religion. In a country that in the past had been ravaged by discrimination, oppression, exploitation and exclusion, and that is now seriously attempting to build bridges among different cultural and religious communities (through its school curricula) I find it ludicrous to think that Muslim learners might be taught to disrespect the other and their otherness. Of course I am not denying that Muslim learners are conscientised to oppose forms of injustice—which happen practically everywhere across the globe—but I cannot imagine that they are actually taught to terrorise people (in retaliation) for perhaps the suffering of some Muslims throughout the world. In the Muslim schools (*madāris*) learners are taught to address any form of injustice through peaceful, dialogical action as opposed to meaningless aggressive retaliation. In South Africa, because of its turbulent political past, Muslims (like many other citizens) have learnt that deliberative engagement is the only option by which to resolve any unfavourable situation. I would be surprised if education officials who regularly visit schools would not have grasped by now that Islamic Studies can be considered to be a gateway for teaching religious extremism in the *madāris* or Islamic private schools—the latter is not the subject of this exploration.

In fact, many Muslim private schools are continuing to grapple with the implementation of the Islamisation of knowledge idea, particularly integrating this concept of knowledge into the curriculum. I have reason to believe that Muslim private schools have not successfully attended to the implementation of this conception of knowledge in schools. Islamisation, though, remains an idea that Muslim schools want to pursue and connect with. And, if this were to be true (and I have sufficient reason to believe that it is), I cannot imagine how Islamisation as a concept can actually 'radicalise' Muslims. Drawing on the seminal thought of the illustrious Islamic scholar of the Malay World, Syed Muhammad Naquib al-Attas (1991), I infer that Islamisation is a conception of knowledge that intends to desecularise education in a non-violent and non-repressive way. Islamisation relies heavily on the logical soundness of arguments, explanation of the meaning of concepts, construction of reasonable arguments, and rational and intuitive reflection that would enable a person to provide philosophically rigorous examinations, critiques, justifications, analyses and syntheses of education. According to Wan Daud (1998: 313–314) the Islamisation of present-day knowledge ought to happen according to two interrelated processes:

1. The isolation of key elements and concepts that make up Western culture and civilisation…from every branch of present-day knowledge, particularly those in the human sciences: He (al-Attas) however adds, that the natural, physical and applied sciences must also be islamised especially in the areas of *interpretation* of facts and *formulation* of theories.…Based upon his (al-Attas's) epistemological and ontological

interpretations of the concepts of *haqq* and *batil* and other related concepts, he arrives at the important observation that not all facts—particularly those that are created by man—are true if they are not in their right and proper places; if they do not conform to the Islamic worldview.

2. The infusion of Islamic elements and key concepts in every branch of the relevant present-day knowledge: These two very demanding (professional) tasks presuppose a profound grasp of nature, spirit and attributes of Islam as a religion, culture and civilsation. Further al-Attas also enumerates and explains some of the fundamental key concepts of Islam which should be infused into the body of any science that Muslims seek to acquire such as the concept of religion (*dīn*), of man (*insān*), of knowledge (*`ilm* and *ma`rifah*), of justice (*`adl*), of right action (*`amāl* as *adab*) and all the terms and concepts that are related to them.

Such an understanding of Islamisation would hardly incite learners to perform acts of violence. If it were to 'radicalise' learners, they would in fact be taught to produce plausible and coherent forms of justifications rather than to learn how to detonate bombs in a marketplace. So, the context of this book is as follows: My understanding of South African Muslim schools (*madāris*)—these are afternoon schools conducted at homes, mosques or buildings designated for the purposes of a Muslim school which usually complements Muslim learners' public schooling that takes place during the greater part of the day; my experience as a *madrassah* teacher; and my ongoing intellectual engagement with contemporary issues about democratic citizenship and cosmopolitan education which have contributed to the framing of this book.

In addition, this book is an attempt to elucidate many different conceptions of Islamic education and some of their interrelated meanings. My main argument is to show that there are—at the least—multiple conceptions of Islamic education which can engender different actions. Put differently, I argue that different conceptions of Islamic education could guide practices in multi-various ways.

In Chapter 1, I specifically explore the concepts of *tarbiyyah* (nurturing), *ta`līm* (instruction) and *ta`dīb* (good action) and show how these concepts are all related to the achievement of truth (*haqq*) and justice (*`adl*).

In Chapter 2, I explicate how actions (`amāl`) such as community (*ummah*), dialogue (*shūrā*) and striving (*jihād*) are shaped differently by primary conceptions of Islamic education.

In Chapter 3, I turn my attention to how Islamic educational institutions such as the elementary school (*maktab*), mosque (*masjid*) and secondary school (*madrassah*) would unfold following different conceptions of Islamic education.

In Chapter 4, I analyse how different conceptions of Islamic education can cultivate peace (*salām*), compassion (*rahmah*), and happiness (*sa`ādah*), thus ruling out the possibility that violence should be associated with Islamic education in *madāris*.

In Chapter 5, I offer an account of some of the challenges liberal conceptions of education pose to normative conceptions of Islamic education and vice versa. I focus specifically on how cosmopolitan education challenges Islamic education and in turn how Islamic education responds to cosmopolitan education.

NOTES

1   During the apartheid years the Qiblah Movement (with some links to Iran) has often been accused of wanting to overthrow the state through revolutionary, violent means. To my mind Qiblah supporters were more daring in their efforts to resist oppression and mostly defended themselves against state aggression. The state was militarily too powerful to have been hurt by a small group intent on escalating the struggle through non-peaceful means—in any case, a position that was at the time in line with the African National Congress's military armed struggle against the apartheid government.

2   Elsewhere I have argued that the current Outcomes based system of education perpetuates the inequalities of the past particularly producing less numerate and literate learners who fail to cope with the epistemological demands of university education. Primarily, OBE stifles learner creativity and imagination.

CHAPTER 1

Conceptions of Islamic education

Before, I analyse Islamic education, I shall have a cursory look at the conceptual framework which guides my investigation. Relying on the metaphysics of meaning (*ma`nā*) and the semantic analysis methodology used by al-Attas (1995), my understanding of a concept (*mafhūm*) Islamic education is that it comprises constitutive rules (*māhiyyah*) and external realities (*haqā`iq*). In other words, concepts of Islamic education are constituted by what makes concepts what they are, that is, constitutive rules (*māhiyyāt*). In turn, these constitutive rules guide the manifestation of external practices (*haqā`iq*). In other words, concepts of Islamic education are guided by 'what' constitutes those concepts and in turn, these concepts give rise to practices that reflect the way the concepts of, in this instance, Islamic education are conceived. What follows from this is that I shall firstly explore constitutive meanings of Islamic education before analysing how these meanings unfold in practices.

Thus, this chapter takes a critical look at three constitutive meanings of Islamic education. I argue that constitutive meanings of Islamic education ought to be considered as existing on a minimalist-maximalist continuum, meaning that the concepts associated with Islamic education do not have a single meaning, but that meanings are shaped depending on the minimalist and maximalist conditions that constitute them. I argue that Islamic education is most appropriately couched as *tarbiyyah* (nurturing), *ta`līm* (learning) and *ta`dīb* (goodness). I then show how these concepts of Islamic education can be linked to achieving truth (*haqq*) and justice (`*adl*)—that is, primary aims of Islamic education.

Three constitutive meanings of Islamic education: Between minimalist and maximalist views

Before I explore three constitutive meanings of Islamic education, I first need to elucidate a minimalist-maximalist interpretation that emanates from the work of McLaughlin (1992). McLaughlin's defence of a communal conception of citizenship education is enriched by his argument that public virtues impact a liberal understanding of citizenship education. For him, virtues of critical rationality and pluralistic justice (that is, justice for every person) are substantial or 'thick' understandings of a communal conception of citizenship education. A 'thin' or inefficient understanding of a communal conception of citizenship education would unfold in the absence of critical rationality and justice in defence of diversity. Similarly, Barber's (2004) pronouncements on strong and thin democracy also enrich an understanding of participatory democracy. If democracy is strong, then such a democracy is highly participatory, whereas thin democracy makes the latter less participatory. Building on this view, a conception of Islamic education is thick or maximalist if deliberations can lead to justice in people's ways of living. On the contrary, if a conception of Islamic education is thin or minimalist, then the possibility of deliberative engagement and justice for all peoples would be restricted. Now bearing in mind that Islamic education can be constituted by concepts that make it either minimalist or maximalist, I now turn to a discussion of those concepts that can have both a maximalist and a minimalist interpretation.

Islamic education can most appropriately be framed according to three interrelated concepts: *tarbiyyah* (rearing or nurturing), *ta`līm* (learning/instruction) and *ta`dīb* (good action). Firstly, *tarbiyyah* (rearing) signifies a process of socialising people into an inherited body of knowledge. This includes teaching Muslims about their faith (Islām), tenets of their faith (belief in the Unity of Allāh Almighty, His Angels, Revealed Books, Prophets, the Last Day of Judgement, and that Allāh commands people to perform righteous acts and to refrain from any form injustice), practices associated with a Muslim's life, belief in the Absolute Unity of Allāh Almighty, performance of prayer, giving of alms to the destitute and poor, fasting during the month of *Ramadān*, performance of pilgrimage to Makkah at least once in a Muslim's life time (*hajj*), if having the means to do so, the *sīra* (life history and example of the Prophet Muhammad) and the *sharī`ah* (law contrived by Islamic jurists for Muslims to live their lives in relation to contemporary societal conditions). On the one hand, a minimalist account of *tarbiyyah* is often associated with the uncritical acceptance of most of the inherited facts about Islām. This implies that knowing *what*, knowing *how* and knowing *to be* get preference without having to know *why*. Simplistically put, a Muslim is reared to know what prayer entails, how to perform it and to be a dedicated performer of prayer. Yet such a person is not always expected to know why he or she performs prayer, thus possibly becoming an uncritical doer of Islamic acts without being expected to question the legitimacy of performing prayer. A person exposed only to a minimalist account of *tarbiyyah* often becomes an uncritical believer who does not bother to question the merits and demerits of his or her beliefs. Similarly, a person commits the Qurān (primary source of Islamic education) to memory and does not bother to understand its meanings. Such a person can be said to have acquired a minimalist view of *tarbiyyah* on the grounds that memorisation of the Qurānic text is pursued independently of an understanding of its meanings. Following a maximalist account of *tarbiyyah*, on the other hand, a person also endeavours to find out the reasons why, for instance, prayer is sacrosanct in the Islamic discourse. Such a person questions, analyses the reasons for these actions and does not hesitate to take the tenets into critical scrutiny. Although he or she is socialised into an inherited body of Islamic facts, she or he can take these facts into systematic controversy. He or she has developed a heightened sense of criticality that does not allow for things to be taken at face value, but rather for the underlying assumptions of beliefs and practices to be questioned.

Secondly, on the one hand, a minimalist account of *ta`līm* (learning) would imply that learners commit volumes of texts to memory. For instance, many Muslim learners have memorised the entire Qurān (primary source of Islamic education) and even countless *ahādīth* (literally sayings of the Prophet Muhammad often dealing with his life experiences). Such a form of learning is basically considered to be self-learning; that is, the individual has committed many facts to memory and often does not put into question the interpretations of exegetical scholars (mostly of the medieval period). Thus, once a person has committed a *Hadīth* (a saying of the Prophet Muhammad) to memory (by rote), such a person would not always challenge the interpretation of the narrative as he or she has encountered it and as it was viewed by a medieval exegetical scholar. In other words, learning in this fashion means that one's interpretations of Islamic education is always subjected to the opinions of the jurists of the past, whether Imām Shāfi`i, Abū Hanīfah, Ahmad Ibn Hambal, or Imām Mālik (the four famous jurists whose works enjoy uncritical support, following this idea of self-learning).[1] This approach to learning is not always amenable to flexibility and adaptability, as the argument is often used that the Qurān and *Ahadīth* (plural form of *Hadīth*) are immutable and cannot be changed.

A maximalist account of learning, on the other hand, does not entirely reject rote learning *per se,* but argues that learning is more a matter of public deliberation (*shūrā*). By this is meant that learning occurs when views are considered to be in the public realm and justifiable arguments are proffered in defence of particular truth claims. This view also holds that no scholar has absolute jurisdiction over what counts as legitimate or not, but rather that meanings are shared, experienced and deliberated upon on the understanding that something new or other might still emanate. There is no closure as far as deliberating views is concerned, because something different and more defensible and perhaps worthwhile might still ensue. Such a view of learning considers learning as deep and not superficial, because new and defensible points of view can only emanate once older and less defensible views are challenged or modified, or even abandoned for more plausible views. And given that learning takes place under conditions of public deliberation, the possibility is always there that views are contested, even to the extent that arguments are offered in slightly belligerent fashion.

Thirdly, a minimalist view of *ta`dīb* (goodness) considers the purpose of Islamic education as being biased towards the Muslim community. This means that Muslims patriotically and at times blindly support other Muslims, because it is narrowly conceived that goodness is only meant for those of an Islamic orientation—Muslims are the only ones who can be associated with doing acts of goodness, for example. This account of education (in a minimalist sense) is connected with a narrow view that the Muslim community should be unfairly prejudiced in favour of any other person.[2] A maximalist account of *ta`dīb* (goodness), on the other hand, considers every individual irrespective of linguistic, cultural, religious, socio-economic, political and ethnic differences as worthy of respect as persons. More specifically, such a view of education demands justice for all people and holds that the ownership of goodness is not the reserved property of any single group of persons, whether Muslim or non-Muslim. Goodness is for society and not Muslims alone, and every person should be a candidate for being considered a representative of goodness on the basis of the acts of justice he or she performs.

Now that I have given an exposition of what a minimalist-maximalist account of Islamic education entails, I shall explore the purposes of these three conceptions of Islamic education. In the following section I argue that *tarbiyyah* (rearing or nurturing), *ta`līm* (learning) and *ta`dīb* (goodness) are aimed at cultivating truthful and just individuals and communities.

Truth and justice as reasons for enacting Islamic education

The Qurān is replete with *āyāt* (verses) that exhort humanity towards truth (*haqq*) and justice (*`adl*).[3] If one considers that the early converts to Islam were persuaded by reasons to see the point of their newly found faith, then truth can be associated with the autonomous agreement about the reasons offered in defence of a particular dogma—in this instance, Islam. It seems inconceivable to associate freedom of belief with coercing people to embrace the canons of Islam. In a different way, truth signifies an autonomous and purposeful volition on the part of Muslims to be guided by the tenets of Islam. And if Muslims willingly and rationally (that is, being informed through reasons) commit themselves to the norms of their faith, then they can be described as being truthful. This was the example of the Prophet Muhammad who willingly declared his faith in the presence of polytheists in his community to the extent that he was persecuted and tormented for his beliefs. Thus, if the purpose of Islamic education is to attain truth, then it follows that such an education ought to engender in Muslims a keenness to practise Islam through reason and persuasion. Small wonder the Qurān distinguishes unequally between the knowledgeable and those people who are not knowledgeable.[4] It was the knowledgeable people who strove to 'seek out the truth', that is, to articulate it (Wan Daud, 1990: 13). What this means is that Muslims strove to articulate truths instead of subjecting themselves to 'all forms of superstitious beliefs and practices like magic, sorcery, astrology, and all varieties of predicting the future' (Wan Daud, 1990: 13). The idea that truth constituted the practices of the early Muslims, as well as its link with knowledge, is supported by a *Hādīth* narrated by Abdullāh ibn Masūd. According to him, the Prophet Muhammad (May the peace and blessings of Allāh be upon him, SAW) urged Muslims to emulate a person who spends his wealth in the service of *haqq* (truth) and acts according to his knowledge given by Allāh. Hence, the attainment of truth is connected with the autonomous search for seeing the point on the basis of articulation, persuasion and argumentation in accordance with a person's epistemological advances.

In addition, one of the early Makkan revelations (al-'Asr), revealed against the background of the polytheistic obsessions of the Qurayshite Makkans, such as their belief in false deities and their adoration of personalities, of wealth, of social status and power, emphasises the importance of truth (Bashier, 1978: 122). The concepts conveyed through this Qurānic revelation were directly applicable to the decadent human environment it was about to transform:

> By al-'Asr (the time). Verily, man [woman] is in loss, except those who believe (in Islamic monotheism) and do righteous good deeds, and recommend one another to the truth (that is, order one another to perform all kinds of good deeds (al-m'arūf) which Allāh has ordained, and abstain from all kinds of sins and evil deeds (al-munkar) which Allāh has forbidden), and recommend one another to patience (for the sufferings, harms, and injuries which one may encounter in Allāh's cause during preaching His religion of Islamic monotheism or jihād) (al-'Asr: 1–3).

The aforementioned Qurānic revelation illustrates firstly the importance of familiarising people with the concepts of faith and righteous deeds. After people had been persuaded through reasons to acknowledge the humiliating and degrading effects polytheistic values had on their intellect and practices, they were encouraged to repudiate these oppressive values in order to attain truth—a situation which seems generally to be linked to early Muslim practices. Some of these Muslims could no longer subject themselves to false deities and false worship. They resigned themselves entirely to the submission of One, Supreme Allāh. By implication, the revelation of this particular chapter (at a specific time in Muslim history when unbelief and polytheism were dominant), primarily to familiarise people with the content of Islamic faith and deeds, points out the coherent manner in which Qurānic guidance was revealed. People were first persuaded to renounce unbelief through reasons before they could submit themselves truthfully to Allāh—that is, a matter of justifying the reasons for accepting the Islamic faith.

In addition, the Qurān also abounds with verses (āyāt) that emphasise the significance of achieving justice for all human beings, wherever they might be. The most famous of these verses is the one that is recited every Friday when the imām (congregational leader) renders the compulsory khutbah (sermon): 'Surely Allāh enjoins the doing of justice and the doing of good (to others) and the giving to the kindred. And He forbids indecency and evil and rebellion; He admonishes you that you may be mindful' (al-Nahl: 90). Again, in another verse: 'O you who believe! Be upright for

Allāh, bearers of witness with justice, and let not hatred of people incite you to act inequitably; act equitably, that is nearer to piety, and be careful of (your duty to) Allāh; surely Allāh is Aware of what you do' (al-Māidah: 8). Likewise, it is stated in the Qurān: 'O you who believe! Be maintainers of justice, bearers of witness for Allāh's sake, though it may be against your own selves or (your) parents or near relatives; if he [she] be rich or poor, Allāh is nearer to them both in compassion; therefore do not follow your low desires, lest you deviate; and if you swerve or turn aside, then surely Allāh is aware of what you do' (al-Nisā: 135). Now considering that the Qurān is one of the primary sources of Islamic education—another being the *Sunnah* or life experiences of the Prophet Muhammad (SAW)—and that the Qurān clearly emphasises the importance of achieving justice for all, it would be plausible to claim that the rationale for Islamic education is the achievement of `adl (justice) in relations among people. What the aforementioned verses also foreground is an understanding that justice is not the domain or proprietorship of individuals, but that justice is done to others and in relation with others. These others, of course, might not necessarily be of the same religious, cultural, linguistic, ethnic, political, cultural or social milieu as the one or the groups enacting justice. Simply put, justice is not reserved for a particular group (such as Muslims), but rather for all people wherever they might live. In this sense, the enactment of justice is a universal or global enterprise.

The question arises: What does it mean to be treated justly? Firstly, justice is conceptually linked to being non-offensive, non-subversive and decent towards others. If so, then one should treat others with dignity and respect without inflicting physical and emotional harm on them. Pedagogically, this makes sense because learning and teaching cannot take place without people (learners and teachers) being made to feel that they deserve one another's respect as dignified persons. Secondly, being just requires of one not to act unfairly (perhaps through bigotry and resentment). In other words, people should be treated equally and no-one should be unjustly singled out as a 'stranger'. I think specifically of the challenges that teachers in some Islamic institutions face not to treat students from immigrant communities, for instance, as if they do not deserve our equal and symmetrical attention. Thirdly, justice is linked to recognising the rights of others (and not just being consumed with asserting one's own rights) and to the assurance of their (others') rights. I think of the rights that learners from all Islamic communities have to education and how teachers all over the world should go about ensuring that their rights to education are secured.

The aforementioned Qurānic understandings of truth and justice advance two things: first, that one has to justify one's claims on the basis of reasons (that is, to offer some account of what one's speech acts entail); and second, that one does so (that is, offer reasons) in a reasonable (or civil) manner. But giving an account of reasons through coherence and civility is conncetd to understandings of knowledge. One's understanding of knowledge (al-Attas, 1991: 34) determines the way one conducts oneself in the community. This brings me to a discussion of two kinds of knowledge in Islamic education and how this knowledge can contribute to achieving truth and justice—that is, how these kinds of knowledge can assist one in articulating reasons and in acting reasonably (that is, with civility). My reason for exploring different understandings of knowledge is grounded in a view that Islamic education *per se* ought to be considered as a practice guided by knowledge concerns. Al-Attas (1991: 34) aptly makes the claim that Islamic education has the possibility of being misguided if attention is not adequately paid to 'confusion and error in knowledge which are all happening among Muslims today'—a view that strongly emphasises the link between Islamic education and knowledge. And, if Islamic education is not guided by appropriate forms of knowledge, it will 'give rise to leaders who are not qualified for valid leadership of the Muslim Community' (al-Attas, 1991: 34). Small wonder, then, that the idea of an Islamic university, following al-Attas (1991: 40), 'must reflect the Holy Prophet in terms of knowledge and right action'. This brings me to a discussion of knowledge in relation to achieving truth and justice.

Knowledge, truth and justice

Broadly speaking, Islamic scholars classify knowledge as revealed (*naqli*) and non-revealed (`*aqli*). Revealed knowledge refers to the transmitted religious sciences such as the Qurān, *Sunnah* (life experiences of the Prophet as captured in the *ahādīth*), *sharī`ah* (jurisprudence and law), theology, Islamic metaphysics (*al-tasawwuf*), and the Arabic grammar (including its lexicography and literature). Non-revealed knowledge includes the rational, intellectual and philosophical sciences such as the human sciences, natural sciences, applied sciences, technological sciences, comparative religion, Western culture and civilisation, linguistic sciences, and Islamic history (including Islamic thought, culture and civilisation, and Islamic philosophy of science) (al-Attas, 1991: 42–43). In his *al-Itqān fī `Ulūm al-Qur`ān*, Jalāl al-Dīn al-Suyūṭī (one of the foremost Islamic commentators), asserts that the Qurān is a Book that contains knowledge of various types of sciences (al-Suyūṭī, 1973: 164). According to him, there is not a branch of knowledge that can be considered as valid without the Qurān, that is, the revealed knowledge of Allāh Almighty (al-Suyūṭī, 1973: 164). It is my understanding that al-Suyūṭī does not deny the validity of non-revealed knowledge. It seems that for him, non-revealed knowledge is in complementarity with the revealed Qurān. In support of this, on the one hand, as confirmed in the Qurān, Allāh exhorts humankind to study natural phenomena such as geo-physical sciences, biological sciences and technology, that is, those non-revealed sciences, whereas, on the other hand, the Qurān claims to be a major source of knowledge itself:

> There is not a moving (living) creature on earth, nor a bird that flies with its two wings, but are communities like you. We have neglected nothing in the Book, then unto their Lord they (all) shall be gathered (*al-An-`ām*: 38).
>
> And (remember) the Day when We shall raise up from every nation a witness against them from amongst themselves. And We shall bring you (O Muhammad SAW) as a witness against these. And We have sent down to you the Book (the Qurān) as an exposition of everything, a guidance, a mercy, and glad tidings for those who have submitted themselves (to Allāh as Muslims) (*al-Nahl*: 89).

My understanding of these verses is that human (Muslim) educative activity in the realm of non-revealed knowledge rests on revealed Qurānic guidance regarding natural phenomena such as embryology, geology, zoology, botany, astronomy, and so on. What this means is that the development of an Islamic educational curriculum integrates revealed Qurānic guidance and non-revealed sciences extracted from it. Hence, there is a harmonious complementarity between revealed and non-revealed knowledge. In this way, Islamic education is constituted by a non-bifurcationist or integral relationship between revealed knowledge and what is considered to be non-revealed knowledge. In this regard al-Suyūṭī (1973: 164) mentions the Qurān as the source from which an understanding of the beginning of creation, the vastness of the heavens and the earth, as well as what is below the earth, can be extracted.

In essence, the Qurān acknowledges the importance of drawing on a variety of non-revealed knowledge in order to understand its guidance (revealed knowledge). Not surprisingly, Abdullah (1982: 134) posits that integrating the different elements (that is, a variety of non-revealed knowledge) is a fundamental characteristic of Qurānic guidance. What this means is that different disciplines such as history, psychology, natural sciences, philosophy and sociology may all contribute to informed interpretations of the revealed guidance. For example, an Islamic teacher can make use of the findings of the psychologists (who study human behavioural patterns) and the sociologists (who study human beings in the context of their environment) in order to interpret the Qurānic guidance regarding human conduct. This is not an indication that the Qurānic guidance is inadequate, but rather, an insightful way of interpreting the guidance. Now that I have shown how revealed and non-revealed knowledge can possibly integrate, I shall examine such a non-bifurcationist view of knowledge in relation to *tarbiyyah* (rearing or nurturing), *ta`līm* (learning) and *ta`dīb* (goodness).

Firstly, *tarbiyyah* (rearing or nurturing) in a maximalist sense implies that learners have to be exposed to a non-bifurcationist view of knowledge. This is so for the reason that a bifurcationist view does not restrict an understanding of knowledge to non-revealed or revealed knowledge only. If so, it would reduce the opportunity of learners to maximise what could potentially be learnt. For instance, when learners are socialised with theological understandings of Allāh's Attributes, these are dealt with in a way that explains rationally Allāh's Divinity. This means that Allāh's Divinity is accounted for and justified on the basis of both its theological underpinnings and the reasons offered in defence of such views. Consider the metaphorical expression in the Qurān of Allāh's 'hand' (*al-Āli Imrān*: 73). The theological conception of 'hand' or *yadd* has to do with Allāh's Supreme Power, whereas a rational explanation is linked to an affirmation of Allāh's laws that govern the universe (that is, *taqdīr*). And, if learners are socialised with such a non-bifurcationist view of knowledge then they (learners) are initiated into Islamic beliefs in a maximalist way. Exposing learners merely to literal understandings of Allāh's 'hand', for instance, could be related to some physical activity which perhaps refers to Allah's 'hand' in a volcanic eruption—here, a minimalist view of knowledge in a theological sense would have been taught. The point about socialising learners with Islamic beliefs is that understandings of beliefs are not just emphasised theologically but that beliefs are also explained on account of non-theological, justifiable reasons. So, for learners to be initiated into beliefs of the Islamic faith often requires the use of revealed and non-revealed knowledge. Similarly, learners can also be taught the rational explanations related to the use of Allāh's 'hand' (for instance, the scientific laws of Allāh that govern creation) and then be referred to a higher form of knowledge (with reference to the Qurānic guidance) to complement rational formulations. Here, I specifically think of the Qurānic injunctions related to the 'destruction of communities' (al-Hāqa: 9 & Hūd: 117), which can be used to understand the annihilation of communities, for instance, as a result of the HIV and AIDS pandemic. The point about socialising learners with the tenets of the Islamic faith through tarbiyyah has a better chance to be realised in a maximalist way if learners are initiated into understandings on the basis of an integrated view of revealed and non-revealed knowledge. Learners' socialisation would hopefully be maximalist in the sense that their reasons would be informed by a complementary view of knowledge. Of course, my potential critic might argue that integrating two kinds of knowledge could result in confusion about Islamic beliefs, for revealed and non-revealed knowledge stand in stark contrast to each other. If this argument were to be legitimate then one would presume that revealed knowledge is unrelated to rationality and in turn, non-revealed knowledge is precluded from having a religious or ethical dimension. On the contrary, my reading of the primary sources of Islamic education is that both the religious and the rational are emphasised in a complementary way. In this regard Muslims are exhorted to consider and marvel about the creation of the heavens and the earth with the utmost of reflection (al-Baqara: 164):

> Verily! In the creation of the heavens and the earth, and in the alternation of night and day, and the ships which sail through the sea with that which is of use to mankind, and the water (rain) which Allāh sends down from the sky and makes the earth alive therewith after its death, and the moving (living) creatures of all kinds that He has scattered therein, and in the veering of winds and clouds which are held between the sky and the earth, are indeed āyāt (proofs, evidences, signs, etc.) for people of understanding.

Secondly, ta`līm (learning), would most appropriately gain extended ground if practised in relation to a non-bifurcationist view of knowledge construction. Why? Learning about revealed knowledge only would not necessarily acquaint learners with reasons that adequately explain scientific events, historical and sociological occurrences and human interactions. This implies that one would not lucidly and defensibly explain natural and human occurrences on the basis of revealed knowledge only. For example, one can account for the origin of the universe on the basis of the Qurānic injunction that creation originated from a gaseous explosion; or that life on earth originated from water; or that human beings are afforded with cognitive capacities to enhance their cooperation. But reasons for the aforementioned actions would only be limited to the overarching rules associated with these processes and not the minute detail related to their unfolding. Thus, one would not be informed through the Qurān, for instance, about the psycho-analytic processes which occur in the human mind or the nature of gaseous explosions. Learning about processes in a limited way only would render such learning less informative and contemplative. However, contextualising and explaining such actions in relation to theories of natural and human occurrences would render more informative and extended explanations. Put differently, using both revealed and non-revealed knowledge to explain natural and human occurrences would produce more informed and reasonable meanings, and in turn, more contemplative learning would hopefully occur.

Thirdly, ta`dīb (goodness) is connected to a process of 'Islamisation' of knowledge which refers to 'the deliverance of knowledge from its interpretations based on secular ideology; and from meanings and expressions of the secular' (al-Attas, 1991: 43). Here, secular refers to a practice that disconnects religious understandings of knowledge from political, social and cultural aspects of life (al-Attas, 1995: 24–25). For this reason, 'Islamisation' of knowledge does not, firstly, separate a study of rational, intellectual and philosophical sciences from a study of religious sciences; and secondly, it extends a study of knowledge to include 'disciplines' such as comparative religion, Western culture and civilisation, linguistic sciences, and Islamic thought, culture and civilisation (al-Attas, 1991: 43). Hopefully, such an 'Islamised' conception of knowledge would countenance a bias towards magic, myth, and cultural traditions (al-Attas, 1991: 46).

What follows from the aforementioned is that a minimalist view of ta`dīb would consider the study only of the Qurān, Sunnah, Sharī`ah, theology and Islamic metaphysics (al-tasawwuf) independent from the human, natural, applied and technological sciences, and vice versa. Also, a minimalist view of ta`dīb would not extend an integrated conception of knowledge, that is, religious with rational, intellectual and philosophical to the study of knowledge about languages, cultures and civilisations. In fact, a maximalist view of ta`dīb would be attained only if a 'harmonious unity' of different kinds of knowledge is emphasised and maintained, and if such a conception of knowledge can in fact contribute to producing a good person—a person who contributes towards the advancement of societal life. In this regard, al-Attas (1991: 25) makes the point that *ta`dīb* is aimed at producing a person who can put knowledge to 'good use in society'. For me, people who are not capable of situating knowledge and becoming people who are responsive to societal issues in a just manner, have not practised *ta`dīb* in a maximalist sense. Small wonder that the Qurān constantly reminds Muslims to do things of value to society and simultaneously to link good actions with the manifestation of truth and justice—thus practising *ta`dīb* in a maximalist sense (*al-Asr*: 1–3).

In this chapter, I have given an account of at least three conceptions of Islamic education, namely *tarbiyyah* (nurturing), *ta`līm* (learning) and *ta`dīb* (goodness) and I have shown how these concepts can be framed on a minimalist-maximalist continuum of Islamic education. My argument for a maximalist conception of Islamic education has mostly centred on three aspects: firstly, the view that a maximalist conception of Islamic education is inextricably connected to a non-bifurcationist view of knowledge; secondly, that a maximalist conception of Islamic education is always situated in actions aimed at achieving truth and justice in society; and thirdly, that a defensible view of Islamic education is more appropriately articulated through *ta`dīb* (goodness) because the latter advocates for the 'Islamisation' of knowledge which would not only connect people to real-life situations but also inspire them to actuate just change.

NOTES

1   In fact, controversy in Muslim communities often arises as a result of people departing from the interpretations of these jurists. It must also be emphasised, however, that these scholars encouraged critical engagement with their thoughts.

2   I am not suggesting that Muslims should not patriotically support other Muslims. However, if Muslims are wrong, one cannot blindly support their actions. For instance, if Muslims are responsible for acts of hostility and aggression, these acts should be condemned. And, those who inflict harm on others should be held accountable for their actions.

3   *Al-`Arāf*: 159, 181, and *Sād*: 26

4   Al-Zumar: 9

CHAPTER 2

Islamic education and practices

In the previous chapter, I argued that different understandings of Islamic education are framed differently, depending on the conception of knowledge that underpins understandings of *tarbiyyah* (nurturing), *ta`līm* (learning) and *ta`dīb* (goodness). In turn, I have shown how minimalist and maximalist conceptions of Islamic education can be framed in relation to the achievement of truth and justice in society. Often understandings of truth and justice in society are linked to an enactment of different practices. In other words, concepts inform and guide practices differently and are themselves reconstituted in different ways. My understanding of Islamic education in terms of a minimalist-maximalist approach is that the former gives rise to practices in distinctly different ways. In this chapter I examine some of the ways in which actions (*`amāl*) such as community (*ummah*), dialogue (*shūrā*) and striving (*jihād*) are shaped differently by minimalist-maximalist interpretations of Islamic education for the reason that the notions of community, mutual engagement and striving are considered as important discourses in Islamic education. I shall firstly examine these concepts in relation to the primary sources before moving on to a discussion of the ways in which minimalist and maximalist understandings of Islamic education can shape such practices.

Ummah as a democratic practice of Islamic education

The Qurān (*al-`Arāf* 181) states the following: 'And of those whom We have created, there is a community who guides (others) with the truth, and establishes justice therewith.' This verse clearly emphasises the connection between community and actions aimed at achieving truth and justice in society. Likewise, the Qurān (*Ali al-Imrān*: 110) emphasises the following: 'Ye are the best community that hath been raised up for mankind. Ye enjoin right conduct and forbid indecency; and ye believe in Allah. And if the People of the Scripture had believed it had been better for them. Some of them are believers; but most of them are evil-livers.' Here, the Qurān links the notion of community to just conduct and truthful action. Hence, the attainment of truth and justice ought to be associated with the notion of community. Al-Rahīm (1987: 10) notes that if people were to fulfil their responsibilities towards other human beings in society they would have to be actively engaged in an unending struggle for the improvement of the economic, social and political aspects of life. He refers to the Qurān (al-Nisā: 95) which states: 'Those of the believers who sit still, other than those who have a (disabling) hurt, are not on an equality with those who strive in the way of Allah with their wealth and lives. Allah hath conferred on those who strive with their wealth and lives a rank above the sedentary. Unto each Allah hath promised good, but He hath bestowed on those who strive a great reward above the sedentary.' Thus, clearly the practice of community is linked with the doing of deeds associated with acts of truth and justice.

Now the question comes to mind: Does community only involve Muslims and, should acting truthfully and justly be only done to Muslims? In response to this question I draw on a minimalist and maximalist understanding of ta`dīb. In the first instance, it is widely accepted by Mulsims that the Qurān, through the Prophet Muhammad (SAW), came to all of humanity and hence community cannot be restricted to Muslim practices: 'And We have sent you (O Muhammad SAW) not but as a mercy for the `Ālamīn (mankind, jinn and all that exists)' (al-Anbiyā: 107). By implication the notion of community cannot be confined to the actions of Muslims. Now a minimalist view of Islamic education, for instance, would emphasise that one can only engage Muslims in the pursuit of truth and justice because as noted by al-`Awwā (in Alibasic, 1999: 292), they are united in creed (`aqīdah). But then, such a view is grounded in an understanding that truth and justice involves only people who are unified in a specific community on the grounds of religion, and that goodness cannot be extended beyond the parameters of homogeneous religious or non-religious boundaries. This view is limited in the sense that truth and justice for and towards people in society cannot merely be based on one's allegiance to the Qurān and Sunnah. One does not have to be a Muslim in order to be recognised as someone who perhaps does justice to people in society. Similarly, being a Muslim does not necessarily assign to one the status of doing acts of justice—one finds many Muslims who remain passive and unconcerned about others in society. In fact, my argument is in defence of a maximalist view of Islamic education that has in mind acting truthfully and justly towards all of humanity. Why? A maximalist view of Islamic education (ta`dīb) involves justice being done towards everyone and not merely confining righteous acts to one's ethnic, cultural, political, literary or religious community. Consequently, one finds the Qurān ubiquitously accentuating the point that truth and justice is for all of humanity and that it is not restricted to particular religious groups: 'O ye who believe! Stand out firmly for justice, as witnesses to Allāh, even as against yourselves, or your parents, or your kin, and whether it be (against) rich or poor: for Allāh can best protect both. Follow not the lusts (of your hearts) lest ye swerve and if ye distort (justice) or decline to do justice, verily Allāh is well-acquainted with all that ye do' (al-Nisā: 135).

Now that I have examined how a minimalist and maximalist view of Islamic education guide an understanding of community, I shall further explore how the notion of community ought to be realised in societal practices. In the previous chapter, I have argued that one of the aims of Islamic education is to produce a good person—that is, a person of *adab*. By implication, the purpose of a community in Islām involves cultivating good persons. And, in becoming good persons, people have to execute the trust (*amānah*) of responsibility towards Allāh and people (that is, Allāh's Creation): 'We did indeed offer the Trust to the Heavens and the Earth and the Mountains: but they refused to undertake it, being afraid thereof: but man undertook it—he was indeed unjust and foolish' (al-Ahzāb: 72). Following al-Attas (1995: 140), such a responsibility entails taking action that is just and proper. More specifically, responsible (just) action 'does not only refer to relational situations of harmony and equilibrium existing between one person and another, or between the society and the state...but far more profoundly and fundamentally so it refers in a primary way to the harmonious and rightly-balanced relationship existing between the man [woman] and his [her] self, and in a secondary way only between such as exists between him and another or others' (al-Attas, 1993: 76). A person who is unjust towards himself (herself) is unperturbed about actualising his or her potential as a thinking and spiritual person and will invariably cause harm to his or her society (Nāyif, 1999: 180). This makes sense, for a person who is unwilling to pursue knowledge, for instance, would remain ignorant about what advantages knowledge would possibly bring to society or not. Similarly, a person who does not care about his own personal development would do very little about societal development. In this way, I agree with the view that justice towards society begins with a recognition and act of justice towards oneself.

Moreover, exercising responsibility towards society as an act of community in the first instance implies that one does not want to see harm being done to humanity. Only then does one act as a member of a community. Of course, a minimalist view of *ummah* (community) such as to reflect Allāh's Oneness and indivisibility, and to realise His will on Earth is onstensibly religious. Therefore, unsurprisingly, many Islamic religious practices are intended to reinforce such *ummatic* ties through reading and memorising the Qurān in Arabic, praying five times a day in Arabic while facing Makkah, attending the Friday congregational prayer services, celebrating the annual *ids* (Islamic festivals), and performing the *hajj* (pilgrimage) to Makkah at least once in a lifetime, if able to do so (Berggren, 2007: 73). However, a maximalist view of *ummah* also extends the practice of community towards a political realm, as noted by Berggren (2007: 73): '*Ummah* is as much a political society as it is a religious community. In other words, Islam is frequently envisioned as a transnational religio-political project for which individual Muslims, wherever they may be, must strive to realise.' To my mind, such a maximalist view of *ummah* (community) is more favourably positioned to enact one's responsibility towards humanity. It is such a maximalist understanding of *ummah* that seems to be more receptive to the cultivation of democratic values and forms of government and to engender uncritical forms of patriotism in society—thus enhancing one's responsibility towards society. It is to such a discussion that I now turn my attention.

Thus far, I have argued that Islamic education in a maximalist sense advocates an integrated view of *ummah*: religious for the individual and political for the cultivation of humanity. This view also accentuates the importance of linking the religious to individual development (although not entirely so, because performing prayer in congregation does develop the social as well) and the political more to the realities in modern society, that is, producing persons who are profoundly attracted to just and responsible action on the grounds of practising democratic values.

I shall now show that a maximalist view of community (*ummah*) can be linked to acting responsibly, that is, democratically in society and its institutions. But first, I need to differ from Ali (2007: 44) who contends that a liberal understanding of Islām with its concerns with democracy, women's rights and empowerment, freedom of thought, and other contemporary issues (such as racism, xenophobia and cosmopolitanism, I would add) is 'unrealistic' and 'irrelevant' to the development of *ummah*. Although I partially agree with Ali that the modernising attempts of several Muslim reformers such as Jamāl al-Dīn al-Afghāni (d. 1897), Muhammad Abduh (d. 1905), Sayyid Ahmad Khān (d. 1898), and intellectuals like Ameer Ali and Rashid Ghannouchi partly ignored many Muslims' illiteracy levels and inability to understand reasons for their lack of development, I disagree with him that the development of community does not require some adherence to democratic ideals. In fact, his own call for communities to use their 'faculties of seeing, listening, and perceiving', to rid themselves from their 'slavish mentality', to be non-violent and transparent, to equalise opportunities for all, and to engage in 'healthy criticism' (Ali, 2007: 67) can be linked conceptually to democratic practices. To my mind *ummatic* practices that are linked to practising some of the ideals of democracy are in fact tantamount to adhering to a maximalist view of Islamic education. I shall now elaborate on this view. In brief I shall show that the practices of a democratic community (*ummah*) are not inconsistent with the primary sources of Islamic education. Firstly, the autonomy to oppose, speak out and criticise (*hisbah*) finds expression in the Qurān and *Sunnah* (Alibasic, 1999: 237):

> And there may spring from you a nation who invite to goodness, and enjoin right conduct and forbid indecency. Such are they who are successful (*Āli al-Imrān*. 104).
>
> Those who, if We give them power in the land, establish worship and pay the poor-due and enjoin kindness and forbid iniquity. And Allāh's is the sequel of events (*al-Hajj*. 41).
>
> The best form of *jihād* is to utter a word of truth to a tyrannical ruler (Ibn Hanbal, n.d.: 1850).
>
> When you see my community afraid of calling a tyrant 'tyrant', then take leave of it (Ibn Hanbal, n.d.: 6531).

The aforementioned verses and sayings respectively entitle people to oppose points of view, to initiate speech acts, and to criticise constructively—all instances whereby viewpoints are taken into systematic controversy, that is, a matter of exercising democratic action. Benhabib (1996: 69) posits that democratic action should be deliberative in the sense that it provides 'a model for organising the collective and public exercise of power in the major institutions of a society on the basis of the principle that decisions affecting the well-being of a collectivity can be viewed as the outcome of a procedure of free and reasoned deliberation among individuals considered as moral and political equals'. In other words, deliberative democratic action implies that a process of public discussion and debate takes place in which citizens and their representatives, going beyond mere self-interest and limited points of view, reflect on the general interest or on their common good (Benhabib, 1996: 69). Democratic action as deliberation also finds expression in the ideas of Walzer (1983: 304), who claims that '[deliberative] democracy puts a premium on speech, persuasion, rhetorical skill...and the citizen who makes the most persuasive argument—that is, the argument that actually persuades the largest number of citizens—gets his (her) way'. Thus, in this regard, Benhabib (1996: 69) pertinently posits that 'the deliberative model of democracy is a necessary condition for attaining legitimacy and rationality with regard to collective decision-making processes in a polity, that the institutions of this polity are so arranged that what is considered to be in the common interest of all results from processes of collective deliberation conducted rationally and fairly among free and equal individuals'. The more collective decision-making processes are approximated through this model, the more the presumption of their legitimacy and rationality would increase. She argues that participation in such deliberation is governed by the norms of equality and symmetry; all have the same chances to initiate speech acts, to question, to interrogate, and to open debate; all have the right to question the assigned topics of conversation; and all have the right to initiate reflexive arguments about the very rules of the discourse procedure and the way in which they are applied or carried out (Benhabib, 1996: 70). Central to Benhabib's exposition of democratic action is the idea that engagement amongst people is guided by openness, (dis)agreement, questioning, debate and reflexivity (that is, temporary decisions can be changed on the grounds of more consideration and evidence)—all deliberative practices which might enhance communal (*ummatic*) practices.

Is deliberation consistent with *ta`dīb*, more specifically a maximalist view of Islamic education? Al-Attas (1991: 24–26) mentions several actions which he associates with *ta`dīb* such as recognition, acknowledgement, discernment, just speech, and 'correct' (appropriate judgement) in relation to oneself and society—that is, the ways in which one engages with oneself and others. In a way, to recognise (or to see the point), acknowledge (respond to what one sees), discern (perceive), speak (articulate) and judge (ascertain) cannot be disconnected from how one engages with oneself and others—a matter of acting in relation to one's own thoughts and those of others. And, when one does so one acts with a sense of respect towards one's own articulations and those of others, and even at times recognises the limitations in one's own articulations. Also, seeing the point and being responsive to the point one makes and those of others and then to judge appropriately is tantamount to acting democratically, that is to say, deliberatively. What follows from this, is that democratic action seems to be commensurate with *ta'dīb*, more specifically deliberation of a reflexive nature. In other words, one cannot appropriately discern and judge if one's articulations are not of a deliberative and reflexive kind—that is, one offers reasons, acts upon one's reasons, reflects about the same reasons and passes judgement about the feasibility or persuasiveness of one's reasons. Small wonder that al-Attas (1991: 25) purports that *adab* (from which *ta'dīb* is derived) 'involves action to *discipline* the mind and soul; it is the acquisition of the good incorrect *qualities* and *attributes* of mind and soul; it is to *perform* the *correct* as against the erroneous *action*, of *right* and *proper* as against *wrong*; it is the *preserving from disgrace*'. To organise one's mindful actions towards appropriateness, plausibility and viable judgement is in fact to act deliberatively and reflexively with one's own articulations and those of others, which might not necessarily be in person or face-to-face, but also as one engages with texts and other sources of knowledge. Of particular importance to *ta'dīb* is the moulding of 'good qualities of mind and soul' which in my view concurs with Benhabib's claim that deliberation should go beyond mere self-interest and limited points of view—a recognition that democratic action is unselfish and expansive with the aim of not merely satisfying the whims and fancies of people. Hence, the view that democratic action is always conducted rationally and fairly—that is, with justice. In essence, I have found Benhabib's position on deliberative democratic action to be quite consistent with *ta'dīb*—the latter being concerned with achieving the lofty ideals of democratic community in a maximalist way.

Secondly, to judge through mistakes—better known as independent juristic reasoning (*ijtihād*)—can be considered to be another practice in Islam that can be associated with the notion of a democratic community (*ummah*) in a maximalist sense. In a famous *Hadīth*, the Prophet (SAW) is reported to have said: 'When a judge making a decision exerts himself and makes a correct decision, he will have a double reward, and if he errs in his judgement, he will still merit a reward' (Sunan Abū Dāwūd, n.d.: 3567). It can be deduced from this *Hadīth* that reasoning though making mistakes is aimed at achieving more plausible decisions, that is, decisions that have undergone greater scrutiny and reflexivity. Two of the most prominent jurists of the Islamic past, namely Imām Shāfiʿi and Abū Hanīfah, respectively stated: 'My opinion is right, and may yet be proven wrong while the opinion of my opponent is wrong but may yet be proven right' and 'This knowledge of ours is a matter of opinion, but is the best we could come up with, and whoever comes up with something better we will accept it' (al-Majīd, cited in Alibasic 1999: 257). Clearly, the notion of *ijtihād* is linked to the method of trial and error which would help people (a democratic community) to discover errors and flaws, and by eliminating them they potentially learn and improve. Popper (1962: 215) makes the point that if contradictions (and mistakes) are avoided then any criticism and any discussion become impossible 'since criticism always consists in pointing out contradictions'. Like Popper (1989: 33–36), a democratic community is advanced by trial and error, by open debate of controversial questions, by conjectures and refutations, and by inviting and welcoming criticism on ways as to how, in this instance, judgements can be improved. Popper (1962: 379) aptly makes the point: 'Nothing is exempt from criticism, or should be held to be exempt from criticism—not even this principle of the critical method itself.' The point I am making is that judging through trial and error should invariably result in a temporary consensus being achieved so that new ideas or viewpoints (that is, judgements) that are more sound and defensible could emanate.

Is *ijtihād* commensurate with some of the practices of a democratic community? Following Habermas (1996a: 299), a democratic community uses consensus as a principle for arriving at more informed judgements on the basis of argumentative communicative action and reflection. In other words, for a democratic community consensus is not regarded as a prerequisite for action, but rather as an agreed-upon decision that reflects the discourse of informed democratic action. Communicative (democratic) action can be considered to be 'unhindered communicative freedom…(which involves) rational opinion- and will-formation'—that is, if an exchange of arguments or points of view in a Habermasian sense were to be unconstrained, then it would follow that no individual or group of people could legitimately exclude others from deliberating on matters that interest them. The rights of people to participate in communicative action are legally institutionalised without any individual being excluded from the political (I would say educational) process (Habermas, 1996a: 147). Moreover, if, according to Habermas, each individual has 'an equal opportunity to be heard' in the democratic process, then democratic action underpins a concern for the inclusion of minority viewpoints and sets limits on what the majority can legitimately do. Of course, Habermas's argument that democratic action must be concluded by majority decision-making does not undermine the views of minorities.

Habermas conceives of majority decision-making as being analogous with reasonableness. For him, the reasonableness of majority decision-making depends on two elements: (1) political deliberation must be concluded by majority decision-making; and (2) the principle of majority decision-making functions as a rule of argumentation requiring minority participants to persuade the majority of the 'correctness' of their views. The point Habermas makes is that *de facto* majority decision-making cannot be the criterion of better and reasonable argumentation, but rather deliberative majority rule 'considered as a reasonable basis for a common practice…until the minority convinces the majority that their views are correct' (Habermas, 1996b: 29). In other words, democratic decisions by majority rule may be revised (and possibly reversed) on the basis that minorities have good reason to question the legitimacy of the majority outcome—a practice that is not out of true with *ijtihād*. Put differently, the future possibility of reversing majority outcomes means that minority views are not permanently excluded from the democratic decision-making process. The kind of majority outcome envisioned by Habermas grows out of a temporary compromise reached between majorities and minorities after agreement could not be negotiated on the basis of deliberation, that is, the majority could not convince the minority of its views and vice versa.

Thus, like *ijtihād,* a discursive account of democratic action endeavours to seek ongoing deliberation in search of the 'better' argument between majorities and minorities after the parties have temporarily reached a compromise for the sake of progress. By implication, democratic action actually compels the majority to take the minority into account; that is, making reasons answerable to minorities. The point is that majority rule should not be abandoned for ongoing debate, reflexive discussion and a means to permanently exclude minorities, but should instead be used as a temporary aggregative procedure of voting to prevent the occurrence of impasses between majorities and minorities. In a Habermasian way, majority rule is a revisable and compromising decision taken not only to ensure that minority opinion is respected—such as the modification of majority views to meet the objectives of minorities—but rather to safeguard open and honest deliberation of an issue before taking a decision by majority vote. Thus the discussion has to shift from the question of the prevalence of simple majority decision-making in deliberative processes to one of what constitutes better and reasonable argumentation. To some extent, Habermas recognises this point: 'In contrast, a discourse-theoretic interpretation insists on the fact that democratic will-formation draws its legitimating force both from the communicative pre-suppositions that allow the better arguments to come into play in various forms of deliberations and from the procedures that secure fair bargaining processes' (Habermas, 1996b: 24).

Certainly, for the practices of a democratic community, Habermas's account of discursive (democratic action) is important, since human beings require deliberation and reflection to convince others of what they have to say. But then, Habermas's (discursive) conception of democratic action assumes that all persons are autonomous and could rationally articulate persuasive arguments through public deliberations. It is here that democratic action, following such a Habermasian view, would not be consistent with *ta`dīb*. In fact, a person of *adab* understands his or her responsibilities towards God, himself or herself and others in society with justice. Such an individual is connected to society. This would imply that individuals might not all be equally autonomous but enter the deliberation with varying understandings of which some understandings would be more developed than others. What follows is that the more autonomous persons would invariably out-argue the less autonomous. Similarly, people do not necessarily deliberate with a concern for justice in society, but rather to demonstrate their perhaps superior oratory capabilities. In this sense their concerns would not be to ensure responsibility towards society but rather for purposes of self-gain and self-aggrandisement. Such a person would not act with a profound sense of *ta`dīb*.

Thirdly, the practice of *ikhtilāf* (disagreement) encourages and legitimises differences amongst Muslims in the interpretation of the primary sources of Islamic education (al-Alwānī, 1994). Al-`Awwā (in Alibasic, 1999: 258) considers disagreement as a legitimate right that cannot be denied people. In fact the existence of different jurisprudential schools of thought in Islam is a manifestation of the practice of *ikhtilāf* (disagreement). Likewise, the most pertinent example that embodies this practice in Islamic history is the Khawārij's (a section of the people amongst whom Caliph Ali lived) treatment of the Caliph when they excommunicated him and debarred him from the pulpit. He nevertheless ensured their freedom of religion, life, property and social security as long as they did not resort to violence. Yet, he only fought them after they took up arms against him. Al-Sarakshi (in Alibasic, 1999: 260) comments on Caliph Ali's excommunication by arguing that there is justifiable evidence that the leader (Ali) encouraged the right of disagreement (on the part of the Khawārij) for as long as the opposition did not embark on armed rebellion, and he claims that their harsh treatment of Caliph Ali did not result in discretionary punishment (ta`zīr). In fact the right to disagree unquestioningly implies the right to freedom of religion, conscience and expression (Kamali, 1998: 315). The Qurān states the following:

> Let there be no compulsion in religion. Truth stands out clear from Error; whoever rejects Evil and believes in Allāh hath grasped the most trustworthy hand-hold, that never breaks. And Allāh heareth and knoweth all things (al-Baqarah: 256).

The aforementioned verse does not only emphasise the importance of freedom of religion and expression, but it also implicitly recognises the right of people to disagree with a religion and to make their own individual choices. Again, the Qurān recognises this freedom as follows: `To you be your religion, and to me my religion (Islamic Monotheism)' (al-Kāfirūn: 6). So, if Allāh offers people a choice about which religion they decide upon, they are simultaneously accorded the right to disagree with a religion otherwise they would not be in a position to choose, that is, to exercise their freedom. In Qurānic verses the following is stated: `We know of best what they say; and you (O Muhammad SAW) are not the one to force them (to Belief). But warn by the Qurān, him who fears My Threat' (al-Qāf: 45); and `And had your Lord willed, those on earth would have believed, all of them together. So, will you (O Muhammad SAW) then compel mankind, until they become believers' (Yūnūs: 99). The point I am making is that the practice of ikhtilāf (disagreement) is a right one cannot deny others to exercise.

Now the question arises: Is there space for the practice of ikhtilāf (disagreement) in a democratic community? Democratic action can be considered to be a form of 'agreeing to disagree' which requires a favourable attitude and constructive interaction with the persons with whom one disagrees. In other words, it consists in a reciprocal positive regard of citizens who manifest the excellence of character that permits a democracy to flourish in the face of (at least temporarily) irresolvable moral conflict (Gutmann & Thompson, 1996: 76). In other words, democratic action requires a 'favourable attitude' even towards those with whom one does not want to engage but with whom for the sake of say, resolving a societal crisis, one declares oneself willing and prepared to engage deliberatively. People ought to engage respectfully in deliberation because they recognise one another's worth as human beings capable of reason and critical reflection, not primarily because of what the outcomes of the deliberation should be. Yet, what also seems to be important for democratic action is that people need to hold others to the intellectual and moral standards they apply to their friends and themselves—'We honor others by challenging them when we think they are wrong, and by thoughtfully taking their (justifiable) criticisms of us' (Fay, 1996: 239).

If people deny others their right to question freely in deliberation, or if others are unable to deal with criticism of their acts, their actions should not be 'beyond the pale of critical judgment' (Fay, 1996: 239)—that is, respect (agreeing to disagree) does not simply mean acceptance of everything people do. Respect conceived as mere acceptance of everything people do or say negates the value of democratic action. This understanding of respect enjoins us to appreciate others but not to engage them in mutual critical reflection (Fay, 1996: 240). Rather, following Gutmann and Thompson (1996: 76), 'mutual respect manifests a distinctively democratic kind of character—the character of individuals who are *morally* committed, *self-reflective* about their commitments, *discerning* of the difference between *respectable* and merely *tolerable* differences of opinion, and open to the possibility of changing their minds or modifying their positions at some time in the future if they confront unanswerable objections to their present point of view' (my italics). Clearly, people exercising a moral commitment towards democratic action on the basis of self-reflection, discernment of judgement, respect and tolerance invariably act with a strong sense of *ikhtilāf* (disagreement).

Moreover, constitutive of democratic action is the practice of freedom of expression, which should not become what Gutmann (2003: 200) calls 'an unconstrained licence to discriminate'—only if one avoids injustice does one act responsibly, that is, 'within the limits of doing no injustice to others' (Gutmann, 2003: 200). In other words, the right to free and unconstrained expression ends when injustice to others begins. One can no longer lay claim to being non-discriminatory and therefore being responsible and just if one advocates a particular point of view that entails excluding certain individuals—that is, discriminating invidiously against others (particularly those individuals in society most vulnerable and who lack the same expressive freedom as those who are excluding them) on grounds such as gender, race, sexual orientation, ethnicity and religion (Gutmann, 2003: 200). So, if people want to be offensive to others, whether it be the Taliban who castigate Buddhists, al-Qaeda who practise anti-Semitism, the Danish cartoonists who caricature Islam's Prophet, radicals who attempt to execute reputable scholars (such as the Egyptian Nobel Prize laureate for literature), or soldiers who humiliate and torture prisoners of war, then their actions cannot be left unconstrained and irreversible. The point I am making is that such unconstrained and irresponsible actions are in fact discriminatory, instrumental, biased and non-deliberative, and do not offer any possibility for democratic action. Only through responsible democratic action can our human educational project become a potent means to prevent insecurity, violence and terror. For this reason, ta`dīb through ikhtilāf (disagreement) is considered to be a means by which to assign everything to its rightful and appropriate place—that is, if democratic action aims to engage others without unjustly discriminating against them or freely insult and ridicule others, then human security, world peace and happiness would remain elusive.

Moreover, of importance to this discussion on the practice of ikhtilāf (disagreement) is the notion of how to respond to people who might ridicule Islam or its Prophet in the name of disagreement. The question is: How does one respond to those who attack symbols of Islam? Once again, the Qurān offers a procedure as to how people ought to engage even with those with whom they might strongly disagree: 'Invite (all) to the way of thy Lord with wisdom and beautiful preaching; and argue with them in ways that are best and most gracious: for thy Lord knoweth best who have strayed from His Path, and who receive guidance' (al-Nahl: 125). Again, the Qurān states the following: 'And they say: None shall enter paradise unless he be a Jew or a Christian. Those are their (vain) desires. Say: Produce your proof if ye are truthful' (al-Baqarah: 111). Clearly the Qurān encourages people to disagree with others and to respond to others' views on the basis of perspicuous argumentation. At no time is aggressive and belligerent behaviour towards others with whom one happens to disagree encouraged. Consequently, I do not find Callan's (1997) view of belligerent democratic action quite convincing.

My interest is in what counts as appropriate argumentation in democratic action. Appropriate argumentation seems to be associated with 'grace'—that is, the ability to be polite, decent, accommodating and forgiving. In other words, intolerance and harshness towards another person might be tantamount to undignified and unforgiving or belligerent behaviour. Some people might not necessarily consider provocation and distress as pleasing and might regard these as being counterproductive to ongoing deliberation. Consequently, Callan's idea of belligerence in democratic action might not necessarily be helpful, pleasing and non-threatening to people. Often being belligerent and distressful during deliberations could result in excluding several persons who might be offended by such actions. In this way, the deliberation might be stunted and the desired results would not be attained. Callan (1997: 211) argues that through belligerence in deliberations, teachers and learners disturb complacency or provoke doubts about the correctness of their moral beliefs or about the importance of the differences between what they and others believe (a matter of arousing distress), accompanied by a rough process of struggle and ethical confrontation. If this happens, he argues, belligerence and distress eventually give way to moments of ethical conciliation, when the truth and error in rival positions have been made clear and a fitting synthesis of factional viewpoints is achieved (Callan, 1997: 212). The difficulty with such a position is that Callan assumes that through belligerence and distress the possibility still exists for the deliberation to continue. What he perhaps does not consider is that belligerence in democratic action has the potential to silence dissent and prevent participants from speaking their minds (for fear of being provoked). In this way, the possibility for democratic action might be thwarted and people would become less willing to take risks that might enhance justice in their society.

Now that I have shown that practices of a democratic community (*ummah*) are not necessarily inconsistent with the primary sources of Islamic education, in particular the notions of autonomous criticism (*hisbah*), independent juristic reasoning (*ijtihād*), and disagreement (*ikhtilāf*), I need to move on to a discussion of another way in which Islamic education can be realised. This brings me to an elucidation of *shūrā* (mutual engagement) as a practice of Islamic education.

Shūrā and 'talking back'

There is ample literature on the application of *shūrā* (mutual engagement) in Islamic practices. Kurdi (1984: 69) posits that *shūrā* (mutual engagement) is understood as 'good counsel and constructive criticism', whereas both al-Fanjārī (1983: 236) and Tahhān (1997: 3) consider *shūrā* (mutual engagement) to be a practice that allows for meaningful opposition. Also, Rahmān (1986: 91) makes the claim that *shūrā* (mutual engagement) as a practice implies 'mutual discussions on an equal footing'. The Qurānic chapter (*al-Shūrā*), revealed at a time when opposition to the Prophet Muhammad (SAW) in Makkah was very severe and Muslims were subjected to humiliating persecution, emphasises the need for Muslims to engage in mutual engagement as far as their affairs were concerned. In fact, the importance of mutual engagement in solving problems is emphasised as follows in the Qurān (*al-Shūrā*: 38): '...[*Wa amr ruhum shūrā bayna hum*] who (conduct) their affairs by mutual consultation [engagement]'. Moreover, during the early Madinan period, Muslims were again reminded to resolve their problems through mutual engagement. The Qurān states (*Āli-Imrān*: 159): '...[*Wa shāwil hum fil amr*] and consult them in affairs of (moment) [engagement]. What is significant regarding the notion of *shūrā* is that the practice is connected to justice ('*adl*); to 'relational situations of harmony and equilibrium existing between one person and another' (al-Attas, 1993: 71–72). Hence, justice is a necessary constraint in terms of which the procedure for *shūrā* ought to be developed. I shall now tease out the link between *shūrā* and justice by drawing on the ideas of al-Attas. Firstly, implicit in al-Attas's (1993: 58) view of order in 'relational situations' (such as *shūrā*), is an understanding that one has to be 'conscious and willing' in one's actions—more specifically in *shūrā*. This means that participants in *shūrā* have to be prepared and willing to listen to each other's conflicting views and differences. In other words, the participants in *shūrā* should be prepared to listen to what others have to say. By implication, they should be patient and tolerant towards one another even if they express diverse views. Moreover, even amidst conflict and severe differences of opinion between participants in *shūrā*, the probability of confrontation would be ruled out by the willingness of both partners in the conversation to talk to each other. What I mean by saying that people should exercise a willingness to engage in *shūrā* through tolerance and patience, can be shown in the light of the Qurān (*al-Shūrā*: 43), which, as I said earlier, deals specifically with mutual engagement: 'But indeed if any show patience [and tolerance] and forgive that would truly be an exercise of...[great willingness] and resolution in the conduct of affairs [*shūrā*]'. In support of this, it is related in a *Hadīth* that the Prophet Muhammad (SAW) said the following regarding patience: "What I have of good things, I will not with hold from you: Whoso would be abstemious Allāh will keep him abstemious and whoso would be independent, Allāh will keep him independent; and whoso would be patient, Allāh will give him patience and no one is granted a gift that is better and more extensive than patience" (al-Nawawi, 1988: 31).

In addition, regarding the notions of 'willingness' and 'consciousness', participants must engage in *shūrā* with an attitude of openness. By this is meant that they should not engage in *shūrā* whereby agreement is a prerequisite. What this means is that one person should not coerce another in accepting his views before embarking upon *shūrā* with him. Hence, agreement in *shūrā* should be a desired goal, rather than a prerequisite. In fact, to coerce people in so far as religious affairs are concerned (which include *shūrā*), is dispelled by the Qurān (*al-Baqarah*: 256): 'Let there be no compulsion [*ikrāha* or coercion] in religion—the right way [*tabayyan al-rushd*] is clearly distinct from error.' The noun *ikrāha* is rooted in the Arabic verb of *akraha*, which means to force, compel or coerce (Cowan, 1976: 823). According to al-Tabatabā`ī (1990: 171), *ikrāha* has the meaning 'to compel someone to work without his willingness'. This understanding not to coerce (*lā ikrāha*), is linked to *tabayyana* (to become clear) and *rushd* (good sense or maturity of mind—that is, to gain insight) (Cowan, 1976: 87). Al-Tabatabā`ī (1990: 171) refers to *rushd* as 'to get out the reality of an affair; to teach the right path'. In other words, the agreement that can be attained through openness, ought to grow out of commonly accepted rational principles, what al-Tabatabā`ī (1990: 171) refers to as 'reason and understanding and not compulsion'. Moreover, the Prophet Muhammad (SAW) also became worried when people rejected Islam. Yet, he was admonished by Allāh not to impose his will upon the unbelievers. The Qurān (*Yūnūs*: 99) states the following: 'If it had been thy Lord's will, they would all have believed all who are on earth! Wilt thou then compel mankind, against their will to believe?'

Secondly, drawing on Al-Attas's (1993: 175) understanding of justice, I support the view that justice exists when 'the relation a thing has with other things in the system becomes clarified and understood'. If I relate such an understanding of order to the notion of mutual engagment, then the latter is not only about one participant proving him- or herself 'right'. Rather, points of view should be clarified and understood. This means that insight should be engendered by the participants in *shūrā* which, in turn, would facilitate an understanding of the issue under consideration. And, for the reason that 'insight' is linked to *shūrā*, participants should lay the basis in terms of which they can be persuaded by more convincing arguments. In this sense, *shūrā* does not only involve one person out-arguing the other person, but, in terms of mutual engagement, that the weight of the other's opinion is considered. Moreover, if the weight of the other's opinion is central to *shūrā*, then participants in mutual engagement should be tolerant of and open towards one another. This claim is supported by a *Hadīth* in which Ibn Abbās narrates that the Prophet Muhammad (SAW) said the following to Abdul Qais: 'You possess two such qualities as Allah loves. These are serenity and tolerance' (al-Nawawi, 1988: 399).

Thirdly, Al-Attas's (1993: 198) idea to redress the problem of 'confusion and error in knowledge' through discernment, insight and constant vigilance provides an important constraint in mutual engagement: the necessity for *shūrā* to proceed with discernment and insight, even if one participant introduces a 'new vocabulary' which is incommensurable with another participant's view. This shows the necessity for *shūrā* to proceed, even if one person (or group) justifiably introduces a viewpoint incommensurable with the prevailing ideas. To my mind, *shūrā* should not happen when any power or institution (or its agents) arbitrarily and irrationally silences, terrorises, eliminates or excludes certain justifiably interested parties from *shūrā* merely because it introduces a new vocabulary into the discourse. The Qurān makes it clear that to alienate a person only because he or she introduces something new is tantamount to ignorance. This is the case of the unbelievers in Makkah at the time of the Prophet Muhammad (SAW). They ridiculed him because he brought a message that contradicted their beliefs. Instead of excluding himself from them, he was called upon by Allāh to be steadfast and patient: 'If their spurning is hard on thy mind, yet if thou wert able to seek a tunnel in the ground or a ladder to the skies and bring them a Sign—(what good?). If it were Allāh's Will, He could gather them together unto true guidance: so be not thou amongst those who are swayed by ignorance (and impatience)' (*al-Anā'm*. 35). In fact, the Qurān strongly advocates mutual cooperation through righteousness and piety and opposes non-cooperative dissension and expulsion: 'Turn ye back in repentance to Him, and fear Him: establish regular prayers and be not ye among those who join gods with Allah— Those who split up their Religion, and become (mere) Sects each party rejoicing in that which is with itself' (al-Rūm: 32). Hence, in addition to willingness, openness, patience and tolerance, other necessary conditions for shūrā include steadfastness, righteousness and piety. In support of this claim, the Qurān (al-Ahzāb: 70) states: 'O ye who believe! Fear Allah, and (always) say a word directed to the Right.'

Thus far I have shown that shūrā is connected with mutually engaging people in an atmosphere of openness, willingness, non-coercion and disagreement. This practice of shūrā seems to be salient in the pursuit of realising a maximalist understanding of Islamic education. I cannot imagine people taking appropriate and plausible actions in society geared towards justice if shūrā were not to be a legitimate practice people embark on. In a way, shūrā seems to be closely linked to the notion of producing people in society who can courageously 'talk back'—that is, participate in democratic iterations.

According to the seminal thoughts of Benhabib (2006), democratic iterations involve something like this: one offers an account of one's reasons, which someone else considers and in turn someone else questions one's reasons to which one can respond. Attending to reasons and critically engaging with reasons often results in the adjustment, modification or even rejection of one's reasons. Others would then be encouraged to agree, disagree or even repudiate one's reasons. This deliberative engagement with reasons is done repetitively; hence, democratic iteration is connected with talking back. Benhabib (2006: 48) refers to democratic iterations as 'those linguistic, legal, cultural, repetitions-in-transformation, invocations that are revocations'. What follows from this, is that Islamic education (in a maximalist way) does not simply mean that one listens passively to what has been taught. Rather, one actively and reflexively engages with meanings to the extent that one's own understandings are subjected to critical questioning by others. This dialogical exchange of meaning making, questioning and alteration of thoughts is proposed as maximalist form of Islamic education. Yet, in some communities being educated in this fashion is not encouraged. For instance, in some Muslim communities talking back is not looked upon very favourably and is often considered as showing disrespect for the other. In such communities listening is encouraged without the possibility that one could repetitively disagree and rebut the views of others, especially religious leaders (commonly known as *ulamā*) who are considered as unquestionable authorities. Instead, it seems as if uncritical listening is considered to be the norm. In such instances, the dominant figures ought to be encouraged to have the confidence in themselves to persuade others through argumentation and to suppress their concerns that talking back would cause them to surrender some of their authority. In fact, talking back presupposes that one recognises the presence of the other, who at least should be considered as a person worthy of being deliberatively engaged with. If not, education would either not be possible or at the very least be unjustifiable. This is so because without talking back the possibility of being indoctrinated is highly likely, which in turn would curb mutual engagement and the development of trust (*shūrā*) to enable one to take risks, thus potentially harnessing minimalist forms of Islamic education. Risk taking has some connection with moving towards the improbable, the unimaginable or the lucky find—those outcomes of Islamic education which stand opposed to the mechanical achievement of ready-made answers. Moreover, risk taking also counteracts the possibility that one can reach a final, completed and blueprint decision. Finality in itself curbs the possibility that there is always something to be learned, discovered, or in the making. By implication, finality would mark the end of a maximalist view of Islamic education.

What follows from the above discussion is that Islamic education (maximally) is about connecting with the other, recognising his or her presence, and creating opportunities for oneself and others to talk back—that is, a matter of practising *shūrā*. If this process of talking back happens routinely the possibility that Islamic education would be engaging and risky might create opportunities for people to accept one another as participants who are mutually attuned to one another. Only then could disrespect and hostility possibly be thwarted. I think here specifically about how people in some Muslim communities are inculcated with a mentality of not questioning the religious authorities, yet the past Islamic scholars (jurists) themselves did not expect later generations to regard their mode of thought and action as immutable and beyond reproach. Unless people are taught to have some public say or debate about the reasons for their actions, to reflect upon and defend their views– that is, to engage, contest, recursively question and offer possibilities about the wisdom of the ancestry—they would not even begin to learn or to talk back. In this instance, *shūrā* would not exist.

Jihād and dichotomous understandings of Islamic education

Thus far I have given some indication of maximalist and minimalist understandings of Islamic education. On the one hand, it seems as if a minimalist understanding of Islamic education can be associated with indoctrination and blind imitation whereby people are not required to think and judge for themselves, whereas, on the other hand, autonomous, rational and just action can be linked to a maximalist understanding of Islamic education (Bagheri & Khosravi, 2006: 94). It is such dichotomous understandings of Islamic education that I shall examine in relation to Islamic institutions in the next chapter. However, I now want to use this dichotomous view of Islamic education in order to elucidate how *jihād* (striving) can be (mis)interpreted as a practice to realise indoctrination on the one hand, and autonomous, rational and just action on the other hand.

Nowadays, *jihād* seems to be associated with holy war and terrorism against a perceived enemy by fundamentalist Muslims (Bilici, 2005: 60). So, in a way, *jihād* is misunderstood and propagated by some sections of the media, particularly in the United States, as violent action practised by some fanatical religious zealots who hold extreme Islamic beliefs (Bilici, 2005: 65). For example, Steven Emerson is a well-known contributor to the growing alarmist literature on Islam and terrorism in the United States. In his *American Jihād* he argues that Islam harbours terrorists and that the 9/11 attacks were carried out by a worldwide network of militant Islamic organisations. He offers a caricature meaning of *jihād* as holy war: 'The jihad, the fighting, is obligatory on you wherever you can perform it. And just as when you are in America you must fast—unless you are ill or on a voyage—so, too, must you wage jihad. The word jihad means fighting only, fighting with the sword' (Emerson, 2003: iii). Moreover, Daniel Pipes, another critic of Islam, claims that 'it is bin Laden, Islamic Jihad, and the jihadists worldwide who define the term, not a covey of academic apologists. More importantly, the way the jihadists understand the term is in keeping with its usage through fourteen centuries of Islamic history' (Pipes, in Bilici, 2005: 63). Implicit in the criticisms of Emerson and Pipes are assumptions that Islamic education in both a minimalist and maximalist frame has induced violence and extremism for the past fourteen centuries. Instead, I shall argue that firstly, *jihād* as depicted in the primary sources of Islamic education cannot be associated exclusively with violent, holy war;

and secondly, that Islamic education in both a minimalist and maximalist way does not necessarily encourage extremism.

Firstly, although the Qurān often uses *jihād* in reference to the act of fighting, it offers a more comprehensive usage of the practice. In fact, fighting is one of several approaches in which Muslims can exercise their responsibilities. Other approaches include *jihād* as striving in Allāh's cause to improve one's morality; and peaceful resistance and perseverance against oppression and tyranny: 'And those who strive in Our (Cause)—We will certainly guide them to Our Paths: for verily Allāh is with those who do right' (*al-Ankabūt*: 69); 'And if any strive (with might and main), they do so for their own souls: for Allāh is free of all needs from all creation' (*al-Ankabūt*: 6); and 'Therefore listen not to the Unbelievers, but strive against them with the utmost strenuousness, with the (Qurān)' (*al-Furqān*: 52). These verses enjoin Muslims to persevere patiently in the face of tyrannical persecution and oppression by the Quraysh tribe in Makkah and engage others through persuasion and speech about Islam (Sāfi, 1988: 30). In fact, the following verses exhort Muslims to fight those who use hostility against them without initiating the aggression:

> Fight in the cause of Allāh those who fight you but do not transgress limits; for Allāh loveth not transgressors. And slay them wherever ye catch them, and turn them out from where they have turned you out; for tumult and oppression are worse than slaughter; but fight them not at the Sacred Mosque, unless they (first) fight you there; but if they fight you slay them. Such is the reward of those who suppress faith. But if they cease, Allāh is Oft-Forgiving Most Merciful. And fight them on until there is no more tumult or oppression and there prevail justice and faith in Allāh; but if they cease let there be no hostility except to those who practise oppression (*al-Baqarah*: 190–193).

The aforementioned verses urge Muslims to oppose the tyranny and persecution of the pagan Arabs and not to coerce people into Islam. These verses simultaneously exhort Muslims to defend themselves against hostility by others. More importantly, as soon as the aggressor ceases with hostility, Muslims are urged to terminate their fighting (Sāfi, 1988: 34). What follows from the aforementioned is that *jihād* cannot be tied exclusively to the execution of holy, violent war, but rather to action that can improve the morality of a person, as well as acts of self-defence against those who perpetrate violence against one. After the immigration of Muslims to Madinah they were given permission to fight against those who declared war against them: 'To those against whom war is made, permission is given (to fight) because they are wronged—and verily, Allāh is Most powerful for their aid. (They are) those who have been expelled from their homes in defiance of right—(for no cause) except that they say "Our Lord is Allāh." Did not Allāh check one set of people by means of another there would surely have been pulled down monasteries, churches, synagogues, and mosques, in which the name of Allāh is commemorated in abundant measure? Allāh will certainly aid those who aid His (cause); for verily Allāh is Full of Strength, Exalted in Might (Able to enforce His Will)' (*al-Hajj*: 39– 40). As has been alluded to earlier, during the period when the early Muslims were still in Makkah (before their immigration to Madinah), the Qurān constantly exhorted them to exert themselves with tremendous effort in disseminating and implementing the Qurānic guidance (*hudā*) in their practices. In other words, they were urged by the Prophet Muhammad (SAW) to perform *jihād*. According to al-Rāghib (n.d.: 99), *jihād* means the exertion of one's ability, which is of three kinds: to strive against a visible enemy, to repel the devil and, to struggle against oneself. Moreover, Lane (1984: 473) defines *jihād* as 'the using or exerting of one's utmost power, efforts, endeavours or ability, in contending with an object of disapprobation'. However, al-Rāghib (n.d.: 99) also explains *jihād* as a practice that articulates an idea (*ra`yi*) or concept (*fikr*). Hence, *jihād* cannot be used exclusively in relation to war or fighting. In my view, *jihād* is also a practice to develop, through tremendous effort, a maximalist view of Islamic education. In al-Burūsiy's (1913: 54) *Tafsīr Rūh al-Bayān*, Allāh's knowledge (*ma`rifatullah*) only becomes transparent through *jihād* –that is, through constant striving. What follows from the aforementioned is that *jihād* (following the primary sources of Islamic education) cannot erroneously be linked to violent, holy war as the Emersons and Pipeses of this world would like us to believe.

Secondly, does both a minimalist and maximalist understanding of Islamic education link *jihād* to extremist, violent action? In a minimalist way, to grow up (*tarbiyyah*), to be instructed (*ta`līm*), and to be disciplined about justice (*ta`dīb*) can take the form of an uncritical acceptance about what one is being told, for instance, about a belief in the Omnipotence of Allah, the Day of Judgement, and the performance of righteous deeds. Without thinking about and judging for oneself what can be understood as righteous deeds might not necessarily result in violent action because indoctrination requires that one only does what one is being told to believe and do. In this sense, even being indoctrinated with Islamic beliefs of right conduct does not endear one to violence. However, for instance, if one were to be indoctrinated about acting violently towards others as a way of realising one's obligations to one's faith, then the possibility exists that one can embark on hostility. But then, such aggressive action cannot be associated with *jihād* because self-defence and individual moral upliftment are not considered as reasons for acting. For example, a Muslim suicide bomber could argue that he acts out of self-defence against imperialist aggression. But then, how does blowing up oneself actually improve one's own individual moral development? The point is that one would not even exist to witness one's spiritual progress. Moreover, to be initiated into Islamic education in a maximalist way means that one is invariably attuned to forms of *jihād* whereby one acts justly towards oneself and others. For Muslims, the self-determination to prevent immorality, backbiting (*ghībah*), defamation, derision and exposing the weaknesses of others are considered as important moral restraints. Thus performing an individual *jihād* would be to struggle for moral self-respect. Such an idea of *jihād* of the self (*jihād al-nafs*) is commensurate with a maximalist view of Islamic education which argues for the refinement and discipline of the (individual) body, mind and soul. Also, *jihād* as doing justice to society whether standing up for the protection of life and liberty, human security and dignity, serving the poor and marginalised, is also in consonance with a maximalist view of Islamic education as *ta`dīb* which argues for the actualisation of justice towards society as a whole. That is, practising *jihād* as the determination to oppose forms of injustice such as global warming, poverty, violence and war, nuclear proliferation, racism and ethnic hatred is not alien to a maximalist view of Islamic education.

In sum: I have examined how the practices of community (*ummah*), dialogue (*shūrā*) and striving (*jihād*) are shaped differently by minimalist-maximalist interpretations of Islamic education. In the next chapter I explore how Islamic education manifested in different Islamic institutions.

CHAPTER 3

Islamic educational institutions

What are institutions? What is the link between conceptions of Islamic education and institutions? In other words, what is the rationale for these institutions in terms of which they organise their practices? These are questions which I need to answer, for the reason that I shall also attempt to uncover later on, conceptions of Islamic education which shaped early Islamic institutions.

Firstly, according to Shalaby (1954: 17), the institution where the Qurān, Ahādīth relating to the Prophet Muhammad (SAW), Arabic grammar, stories of Prophets, reading and writing were taught, is the *maktab*. This *maktab* is different from the House of al-Arqām, where the early Muslims received their quality of training. Bashier (1978: 143) describes the House of al-Arqām as 'a sort of School out of which the best cadres of nascent Islam graduated'. It is my contention that the House of al-Arqām was rather a *majlis*, that is, a place where discussion, teaching and learning activities took place (Makdisi, 1981: 11). Moreover, according to Makdisi (1981: 19), the *maktab* became known as 'the institution of learning where elementary education took place and the studies which led to the level of higher education, such as specialization in law'. For him, the *maktab*[1] was recognised as an elementary school where '*khatt*, calligraphy or writing...[was] taught, as well as the Koran, the creed (*i`tiqād*) and poetry' (Madisi, 1981: 19). This claim is supported by Tibawi (1976: 26) who asserts that 'teachers...receive[d] pupils in special places possibly a room in a house...for instruction...known as *maktab* or *kuttāb*, both derived from the Arabic root "to write"'. This idea of the *maktab* as having been an elementary school is vindicated by the fact that learners entered the school at the ages seven to ten (Makdisi, 1981: 19), and were placed under the care of the *mu`allim* (the most common term used to designate the teacher of pupils at elementary level). According to Makdisi (1981: 19), studies of the *maktab* led to study in a *masjid-college* or *madrassah* (the focus of this book) and to the *halqas* of the *jām`i*.

Secondly, after the arrival of the Prophet Muhammad (SAW) in Madinah, the first mosque in Islam (*Masjid al-Qubā*) was erected. The mosque became the major institution in Islam for the dissemination of Islamic education. The importance of the mosque as an Islamic institution for the dissemination of Islam cannot be denied. It was used as a political and cultural centre, a court of justice, an educational institution and above all as a place of worship (Shalaby, 1954: 48). For this reason, the mosque is considered to be the 'first institution of learning' (Makdisi, 1981: 10). Makdisi (1981: 17) identifies two types of mosques. Firstly, there was the congregational mosque or *jām'i* which had *halqas* (study circles). According to Shalaby (1954: 216), 'the teacher usually seated himself on a...cushion against a wall or pillar...[while] the audience formed a circle in front of him'. At these *halqas,* or what Makdisi (1981: 12, 17) refers to as 'institution(s) of learning', various Islamic sciences were taught. Secondly, the everyday *masjid* 'existed as colleges in Islam' (Makdisi, 1981: 21). Such '*masājid*' (mosques), which belonged mostly to the 8th and 9th century, were used for the teaching and learning of 'Islamic sciences and their ancillaries, including grammar, philology and literature...before the advent of the *madrasa (madrassah)*' (Makdisi, 1981: 22).

The *madrassah* developed in the 10th century and flourished in the 11th century (Makdisi, 1981: 28). According to Makdisi (1981: 27), 'the *madrasa [madrassah]* was the Muslim institution of learning par excellence...a natural development of the *masjid*'. In fact the famous Shafi'i Nizāmiyyah Madrassah was founded in 1067 (Makdisi, 1981: 34). What was the difference between mosques and schools? The special material features by which schools can be distinguished from mosques are described by Shalaby (1954: 56) as follows:

> *Iwān*—an ancient equivalent of the modern lecture-room—was the most conspicuous feature to schools. Next come the residential quarters which appeared in most of the school buildings...Moreover the number of the regular students in a school was often limited, and school endowments always mention grants to students.

Makdisi (1981: 34) also distinguishes between mosques and schools. For him, the staff of a mosque consisted of an *imām* (leader of the prayers), whereas the staff of a school consisted of at least a *mudarris* (teacher). In fact, according to him, the early *madrassah* developed several variations: '(a) the double *madrasa*; (b) the triple *madrasa*; (c) the quadruple *madrasa*; (d) the *madrasa* with a *masjid*; (e) the *madrasa* with a *jami'* (Makdisi, 1981: 34).

Besides the *maktab/kuttab*, *masjid* and *madrassah*, there were also other institutions of learning and teaching such as the *khān* (as an 'inn' to be used for private teaching and tutoring), as well as libraries, known as '*bait al-hikma, khizānat al-hikma, dār al-hikma, dār al-'ilm, dār al-kutub, khizānat al-kutab*, and *bait al-kutub*' (Makdisi, 1981: 24–25). In the light of the differences that existed between the *maktab*, the mosque and the *madrassah*, the question might be asked whether these institutions differed with regard to their empirically observable features only. The answer is no, which is evident from the historical evolution as described above. By implication, what makes institutions different from each other cannot just be explained in terms of empirically observable factors: rather 'they [institutions] are [what they are] at any time of their existence because of the quality of thought [I would argue, the understanding of Islamic education] of their members' (Makdisi, 1981: 187). In essence, institutions differ in the way the members themselves conceive them, that is, they differ in terms of their understanding of Islamic education, whether in minimalist or maximalist ways. What this means is that they could have the same external features, but their underlying rationales (concepts) may differ. It follows from this that institutions differ with respect to the understanding in terms of which they organise their practices. Whatever the similarities between them in terms of external features (patterns), institutions differ with respect to the constitutive meanings of Islamic education. Having shown how institutions differ in terms of different reasons of Islamic education their members have, my next move would be to explicate how practices are linked to institutions.

Practices and institutions

Thus far, I have shown how concepts of Islamic education are linked to practices and institutions. Taylor (1985: 34) aptly points out that institutions are the 'stable configuration(s) of shared activity' (or practices), that is, 'certain patterns of dos and don'ts'. This link between practices and institutions is also identified by Griffiths. He asserts that 'we cannot think whatever we like, and we cannot do whatever we like, and in consequence these are limits on what institutions are possible, and surprises about what institutions become actual. The limits of possibility are set by the (cultural and not merely logical) limits of thought, and by the (physical, cultural, social, economic, etc.) limits of practice (Griffiths, 1965: 188).

My emphasis is on what Griffiths refers to as 'physical limits of practice' and the 'cultural limits of thought'. If I refine what I think Griffiths means by institutions, it follows that an institution ought to be constituted in terms of 'physical limits of practice', that is, external patterns which are exclusive to an institution. For example, the reading of the Qurān and the studying of Islamic knowledge are 'patterns' or social practices enforced in a *maktab*—that is, a particular institution. Also, one's understanding of an institution is shaped by the 'cultural limits of thought'—that is, the underlying rationale (or reasons) that distinguishes one institution from another. For example, a *maktab* is different from a *madrassah* for the reason that the 'thought' or reason which shapes a *maktab* differs from that which shapes a *madrassah*. Thus, one cannot assume any understanding of Islamic institutions without uncovering the meanings which constitute institutions' practices. The meanings of institutions are shaped by their practices and reasons. Consequently, institutions and their practices are shaped by particular reasons. This crucial point is noted by Taylor (1985: 35), who claims that 'all the institutions and practices by which we live are constituted by certain distinctions and hence a language which is thus essential to them'. By implication, to assume that any *madrassah*, for instance, is an institution associated with extremism requires some understanding of the constitutive meanings of Islamic education which guide the practices of such a *madrassah*—an issue I shall explore later on in this book. To sum up: I have shown how reasons constitute socially established practices and institutions. Then, particular practices are exclusive to particular institutions, for the reason that both practices and institutions are determined by the reasons which constitute them.

Now that I have established the links between concepts (reasons), practices and institutions, I shall attempt to show some of the ways in which understandings of Islamic education manifested historically in the early *maktab*, mosque and *madrassah*. In this way, I hope to illustrate how the practices in an institution are shaped by their constitutive reasons.

Maximalist views of Islamic education in early Islamic institutions

Order and flexibility in institutions

I shall now look at the way order and flexibility manifested themselves in Islamic education practices in the early *maktab*, mosque and *madrassah*. Firstly, Tibawi (1976: 243) purports that Islamic learning in the early *maktab* was 'concerned with the (D)ivine (R)evelation, its understanding and its propagation by teaching and preaching'. In fact, the necessity for understanding the Qurān on the part of the early Muslims was a Divine injunction which constituted their practices. During the height of opposition to Islam in the Makkan phase, *al-Rūm* (30: 29) was revealed, exhorting Muslims to understand the Qurān: '(Here is) a Book which We have sent down unto thee, full of blessings, that they may meditate on its Signs, and that Men of understanding may receive admonition.' Secondly, with regard to Islamic education in the early mosques (during the post-Prophetic period), Tibawi (1976: 27) claims the following: '[In] the circles of learned men, usually held in mosques…discourse, question and answer were the received method.' Shalaby (1954: 53) also points out that in these mosques, critical interpretation—what he refers to as 'exegesis' of the Qurān and Sunnah—became the order of the day. Thirdly, as has already been mentioned, the institution of al-Nizāmiyyah in Baghdad (Iraq) emerged as an important *madrassah* in the Islamic empire. Subsequently, many other *madāris* (plural of *madrassah*) were established by its founder Nizām al-Mulk. Shalaby (1954: 58), drawing on al-Subki, claims that Nizām al-Mulk had a school built in each town of al-Iraq and Khurasan. Moreover, it is claimed that al-Nizāmiyyah *madāris* 'were always of high standard as they were staffed by the best scholars of the time' (Shalaby, 1954: 140). One of the most reputable teachers at al-Madrassah al-Nizāmiyyah in Baghdad during the 5th century was al-Ghazzāli (Tibawi, 1976: 30). For this reason, I shall look at some of the educational views of al-Ghazzāli in order to uncover some of the constitutive features that shaped Islamic education in the early *madrassah* in Islam. For al-Ghazzāli, Divine Guidance and intuitive experience allow scope for 'rational thinking, logical deduction and empirical observation' (Tibawi, 1976: 41). This means that the learning of Qurānic guidance does not occur separately from an understanding thereof.

For al-Ghazzāli, a learner had to be encouraged 'to use his own sense and judgement and not merely to imitate his teacher' (Shalaby, 1954: 146)—that is, an indication of practising Islamic education in a maximalist way in the early *madrassah*.

In addition, Makdisi (1981: 99–104) posits that the methodology of learning in the early institutions included memorisation, repetition, understanding, *mudhakkara* (reasoning, understanding, reflection and contemplation) and notebook writing. He claims that memorisation, for instance, was not meant to be only 'unreasoning rote learning…(but) was reinforced with intelligence and understanding' (Makdisi, 1981: 103)—thus practising Islamic education in a maximalist way. He mentions the names of several early scholars (as teachers in institutions) such as al-Bukhāri, Muslim and Ahmad bin Hanbal who achieved extraordinary feats in their memorisation and understanding of thousands of traditions (Makdisi, 1981: 100). Other names include:

1. Abul Hasan al-Tamimi (d. 918), a jurisconsult who defended Shāfi'i fiqh, 'then a new method going beyond the techniques of rote memory associated with (H)adīth, to that of analysis and understanding' (Makdisi, 1981: 99);
2. Abū Amr bin al-Alā, for whom 'the first rule of learning is silence; the second, good questioning; the third, good listening; the fourth, good memorising; and the fifth, propagating the knowledge acquired among those seeking it' (Makdisi, 1981: 102); and
3. al-Tabari (d. 923), who is reported to have 'made a strong plea for the acquisition of religious knowledge and its understanding (*tafaqquh*), and censured those of his fellows who limited themselves to transcribing or note-taking without troubling with studying and understanding what they had written' (Makdisi, 1981: 103).

What is clear from the learning of Islamic education in the early *maktab*, mosque and *madrassah* is that the learning was systematic, reflective and imaginative—that is, attuned to a maximalist understanding of Islamic education. The order of Islamic learning involved the learning of facts such as acquainting the early Muslim learners with the facts of Qurānic guidance and the Sunnah. However, this process did not occur independently from the learning of skills such as understanding the facts. Makdisi (1990: 2002) aptly accentuates the crucial role memorisation played in the early days of Islam:

> Memorization involved great quantities of materials, their understanding, and their retention through frequent repetition at close intervals of time. When limited to mere transmission, memorization was simply the attribute of the common man among the men of learning, e.g. the (H)adīth scholars, the lexicographers. Above this rudimentary level...(t)he road to creativity called for progression from authoritative reception and transmission, *riwāya*, to understanding the materials transmitted, *dirāya*, and finally, with personal effort pushed to its limit, *ijtihād*, to creating one's personal ideas, in one's own words, in an elegant style, expressed with eloquence [my italics].

Hence, Islamic education as a practice in the early institutions involved the acquisition of brute data and skills in an orderly and creative way, in terms of which learners knew how to act meaningfully. In other words, following the rule of Islamic education was a condition of meaningful language use. The fact that they had understanding prompted them to do certain skilful things such as to think logically and rationally, to observe and to interpret—all a matter of, in the words of Ryle (1949: 436) 'learning how to do'—or, what I would refer to as practising Islamic education in a maximalist way. Furthermore, following Rorty's (1988: 45) distinction between 'socialisation' and 'individuation' it can be claimed that Islamic teaching involved initiating (socialising) learners into Islamic understanding by encouraging them to memorise and learn basic Islamic precepts—that is, a matter of performing *ta`līm* in a maximalist way. But, simultaneously, the creativity of Islamic education involved a process whereby learners were encouraged to challenge and question, referred to by Rorty (1988: 46) as 'stimulating imagination' (individuation). In the light of Rorty's distinction, for learners to be socialised into received ideas hinged on an understanding that teachers knew how to do it—that is, they did not only know content, but also knew how to impart it. They possessed the skills to do so. In essence, Islamic education in the early institutions was constituted by both socialisation and individuation, knowing content and having skills. What follows from the aforementioned is that *tarbiyyah* (nurturing) and *talīm* (instruction) were extended, so it seems, to maximalist spheres of Islamic education.

The question now arises: How does order and flexibility link up with an articulation of truth and justice? In a different way: How does Islamic education in early institutions relate to *ta`dīb* (just action)? Firstly, I have already alluded to an articulation of truth as that practice which conforms to the requirements of what is 'right'. And, considering the fact that Islamic education is a practice which also involves socialisation (that is, the initiation of Muslims into the revealed or 'right' knowledge/facts), an articulation of truth implies that Muslims have to conform to the revealed knowledge of Allāh—the primary source of Islamic education. Secondly, I have used al-Attas's conception of justice which links 'everything' to its 'right and proper place'. By implication, the practice of articulating justice is constituted by what is 'proper', that is, a sense of coherence, pattern or order. In this way, to articulate justice means to take into consideration what is the most suitable or appropriate for a particular context. Implicit in such an articulation of justice, is to take into account the notion of flexibility. In other words, an articulation of justice implies that one has to create scope for flexibility in making Islamic education (through individuation, that is, challenging and questioning) 'proper' or orderly for changing circumstances.

Variety in institutions

I have already mentioned that in the early *maktab*, Islamic education involved not only the learning of the Qurān and Ahādīth, but also, as claimed by Hitti (1970: 408), 'reading, penmanship…Arabic grammar, stories about the Prophets—particularly *hadiths* related to Muhammad (SAW)—the elementary principles of arithmetic, and poems'. In addition, in the early mosques of Madinah and Basra, 'literary circles' were conducted, Arabic poetry was taught, as well as theology, '(e)xegesis, traditions, jurisprudence and astronomy…[and] even medicine' (Shalaby, 1954: 53). In fact, Caliph Umar is reported to have devised a curriculum for mosque circles which, besides the teaching of the Qurān and Ahādīth, also included 'swimming, horsemanship, famous proverbs and good poetry' (Shalaby, 1954: 22).

Furthermore, for al-Ghazzāli the *madrassah* curriculum may comprise 'many branches' of Islamic learning (Shalaby, 1954: 146). His own Islamic education included learning the Qurān and Ahādīth, listening to stories about saints, memorising mystical love poems, jurisprudence, theology, and philosophy (Bakar, 1992: 157). He makes a clear distinction between revealed sciences—which include a study of Divine Unity, prophethood, eschatology, linguistics, Qurānic interpretation, Ahādīth, jurisprudence, religious rights, transactions and family law—and 'non-revealed' sciences— such as arithmetic, geometry, astronomy, music, logic, medicine, meteorology, mineralogy, alchemy, ontology, God's essence and relation to the universe, prophecy and sainthood, dreams and theurgy (Bakar, 1992: 207–209). Hence, the early institutions recognised the learning of a variety of sciences.

The question now arises: Why was the teaching and learning of Islamic education in the early *maktab*, mosque and *madrassah* in keeping with a maximalist view of Islamic education? Already I have expounded on the role of the teacher as one who socialised and individualised pupils into Islamic education. In addition, Islamic practices in the early institutions also involved, to use Ryle's phrase, 'learning to be'. For Ryle (1949: 444), 'learning to be' involves 'to be honourable', 'to be self-controlled' and 'to be considerate'. This is precisely what the early Muslim teacher did. Bashier (1978: 144) claims that the early Muslims received their 'training' in the *maktab*, and 'strove to apply the Qurānic guidance to their every-day affairs'. Regarding the notion 'to be' in relation to teachers in mosque circles, Shalaby (1954: 25), who draws on Ibn Abd al-Rabbih, narrates a conversation between a companion of the Prophet Muhammad (SAW) and the teacher of his sons: 'The first thing to start with in educating my sons is to improve your own manners. My sons will be deeply influenced by you and will favour what you do and abhor what you avoid.' This points out that the role of teachers in the early *madāris* was shaped by a notion of 'to be', that is, to enact their learning. Likewise, regarding the rationale that shaped the position of teachers in the early *madrassah*, al-Ghazzāli (in Hajaltom, 1982: 29) states the following: '(I)f anyone wishes to acquire for his mind the virtue of generosity (*al-jud*), he should take pains to engage in some action that is generous, such as giving away some particular thing that he possesses. And he should not cease to be interested in this giving until he has fully entered into the spirit of it and has actually become generous' [my italics].

Hence, the role of the teacher in cultivating Islamic education in the *madrassah* was about teaching 'to be' in order that learners can extend such qualities of learning to their societal contexts—a matter of exercising *ta`dīb* (just action) in a maximalist way. Shalaby (1954: 146), drawing on al-

Ghazzāli, aptly describes the role of the Muslim teacher in the early *madrassah* as one who supported 'his precepts by practice' and who taught 'by his reputation', a matter of teaching 'to be'. In this regard, Husain and Ashraf (1979: 104) describe the position of the *madrassah* teacher as follows:

> He was expected to treat his charges not as so many sheep or cattle which needed to be herded, or disciplined, but as impressionable human beings whose characters were to be moulded and who were to be initiated by him into the moral code which society cherished. For this reason in Islam the teacher was required not only to be a man of learning but also to be a person of virtue, a pious man whose conduct by itself could have an impact upon the minds of the young. It was not only what he taught that mattered; what he did, the way he conducted himself, his deportment in class and outside, were all expected to conform to an ideal which his pupils could unhesitatingly accept.

Thus it is clear from the aforementioned that the early Muslim teacher also served as a model to his learners. It is my contention that this model practice of the teacher was entrenched in a particular self-understanding— one which expresses and defends, in the words of Wan Daud (1990: 102), 'what is true, just and humane'. Therefore, Bashier (1978: 144) refers to the first teachers as people who have achieved 'a degree of excellence', a spiritual and moral 'inward force', and a 'dynamic spirit' which transformed their practices in accordance with a maximalist view of Islamic education. Even the teachers of the early mosque circles are referred to as people with 'moral and intellectual qualities' imbued with 'self-respect, modesty and sincerity' (Shalaby, 1954: 24, 164). Moreover, a *madrassah* teacher of the first *madrassah*, al-Ghazzāli (as mentioned earlier), regarded as an 'outstanding jurist, theologian' is described as having himself attained 'the highest level of spiritual realization' (Bakar, 1992: 155, 164). By implication, these early Muslim leaders and teachers developed dispositions and practices in accordance with the guidance of the Qurān and the Sunnah.

The question now arises: How would institutions be affected if an articulation of truth and justice is lacking in the practices of people, that is, if a minimalist view of Islamic education is practised? My contention is that Islamic education practices and their institutions would become impoverished. More specifically, they would probably practise a minimalist view of Islamic education, because a lack of an articulation of truth and justice would give rise to a restricted meaning of Islamic education—one, to use Taylor's (1985: 205) notion, of which 'the original rationale may be lost'.

Al-Attas (1993: 74, 99) claims that Islamic education without *hikmah* (wisdom) and order leads to 'confusion and hence to injustice'—what I would refer to as a minimalist view of Islamic education. He defines injustice as the opposite of justice, which is 'putting a thing in a place not its own; it is to misplace a thing; it is to misuse or to wrong; it is to exceed or fall short of the mean or limit; it is to suffer loss; it is deviation from the right course; it is disbelief of what is true…to repudiate the truth' (al-Attas, 1993: 73). It is this view of 'confusion' which means to 'misuse', to deviate from the right course, to distort the truth, Rahman (1982: 27) refers to as the repudiation of 'more reasonable views'. And, if Islamic education is practised minimally, such a view potentially leads to 'disorder' or 'corruption of knowledge' (al-Attas, 1993: 103)—the 'manifestation of the occurrence of injustice'.

Now that I have examined how a maximalist view of Islamic education manifested in the early Islamic institutions, I shall investigate to how instances of contemporary Islamic thought might have become 'corrupted' and moved along a continuum of minimalist and maximalist views of Islamic education—with at times, minimalism gaining preference over maximalism and vice versa. My reason for this move is based on an understanding that many practices of influential Islamic movements and organisations in particular are reflected in the Islamic institutions to which they are affiliated. This includes mosques and *madāris*. So, investigating instances of contemporary Islamic thought would give one some indication as to what transpires in Islamic institutions. For purposes of this investigation, I have selected regions where the Muslims are in the overwhelming majority, such as South Asia, Southeast Asia, and Turkey, as well as South Africa where, firstly, Muslims are in a minority, and (as I shall show) secondly, that Islamic education institutions, focusing specifically on the *madāris* have links with Egypt, Saudi Arabia, Iran and Southern Asia.

Islamic thought in South Asian *madāris*

In the main *madāris* in India and Pakistan have continued along the tradition of Nizām al-Mulk as it existed in 11th century Baghdad. They have always served as centres for the training of theologians; hence they are called 'religious schools' (*dīni madāris*) (Leiser, 1986: 18). Despite the early focus on rational sciences with Islamic law coupled to 'a science of disputation (*ilm al-khilāf)*', logic, philosophy and Arabic in *madāris,* theology came to dominate these institutions in the 19th century and *madāris* were transformed into institutions exclusively for religious learning and the concomitant emerging Sunni schools of thought such as Deobandism, Barelwism, Ahl al-Hadīth, Shi`ites and Jamāt al-Islāmi (Metcalf, 1982). These schools appealed to specific social groups and were tied to particular regions, which increased the religious and social complexity of South Asia, particularly in the light of 'law, devotional mysticism, and prophetic tradition [which] determined their different [social] orientations' (Malik, 2006: 107). Moreover, the modernist Aligarh school attempted to anglicise the Islamic educational system and was vehemently opposed by the Council of Religious Scholars (Nadwat al-Ulama, established in 1893) which aimed at integrating religious and secular education (Malik, 2006: 107). Some of the *madāris* which did not subscribe to this integration agenda were marginalised but continued to provide knowledge to the majority of Muslims (Malik, 2006: 107).

In the 20th century, by far the majority of the *madāris* (more specifically religious schools) became the target of state reforms aimed at integrating Islamic education with the overall education systems in the region, because they functioned as independent schools financed through private donations (Malik, 2006: 108). These *madāris* have not only played an important role in the dissemination of knowledge but also have a considerable moral impact on local cultures and politics (Malik, 2006: 110). Through efforts of their *ulama* (religious scholars), *madāris* adapted their curricula with minor alterations such as adding subjects from the formal primary education system to their own syllabus. The *ulama* began to exercise more influence on government policy and were also given opportunities to be integrated into the job market: 'Religious schools [*madāris*] do not only have important social, cultic, educational, and economic functions and significance...they are of quite some importance in areas pertaining to internal and external politics as well' (Malik, 2006: 114). Of course, many of the graduates of the *madāris* failed to find employment in the cities, an area neglected by governments in this region, which resulted in thousands of unemployed mullahs (religious leaders) who have access to the masses not being successfully integrated into society. More importantly, following this lack of integration within society 'the bearers and protagonists of various Islamic traditions have taken self-defensive and isolationist, albeit radical positions'

(Malik, 2006: 116). Now if integration of traditional and modern curricula happened and this integration was in fact supported by several *ulama* it cannot be concluded that Islamic education has not been practised in a maximalist way because the latter requires that the bifurcation of knowledge be transcended—a situation which seemed to have occurred in this region. In fact, by far the majority of students in the *madāris* is said to have played a 'quietist role'—that is, a pacified role which was determined by devotional mysticism, law and prophetic tradition as religious repertory to make sense of the predicaments people are facing in a highly fragmented society (Malik, 2006: 117–118).

In fact, the fragmentation of society has not been instigated by joblessness alone, but has also been compounded by the fact that several Deobandis, Barelwis and Shi'ites students and graduates who come mostly from rural and tribal areas where poverty is rife 'are infrastructurally and economically not at all or only partially developed and where the parceling of land has produced a few large land-holders and huge masses of small landholders and peasants' (Malik, 2006: 112). Often from these communities, foot soldiers in the Cold War in Afghanistan were forcefully recruited from amongst young children in *madāris* and refugee camps known as *mujahidīn* and Taliban to retain control of the region for economic and political purposes (Malik, 2006: 117). But then, some students (a minority from the 8 000 *madāris* and almost 3 million students) are instigated by middle-class and secularly educated men to join the terrorist activities of Lashkar-e Tayyiba and Jaish-e Muhammad who have made the regional conflict and those in Kashmir and Palestine their reasons for a militant *jihād* (Malik, 2006: 117). Of particular importance to my argument is the fact that the *'jihādis'* do not embark upon militancy and terrorism as a corollary of an integrated maximalist view of Islamic education as has been alluded to earlier, but rather because of unfavourable material conditions in the form of unemployment, lack of property ownership, ongoing regional/tribal conflict which seem to be exacerbated by state indoctrination, especially in Pakistan: 'The dramatic flaunting and celebration of military power on national occasions such as Pakistan Day, the propagation of *jihād* in textbooks even in formal schools and daily on television for the cause of Kashmir, etc. are cases in point. This state-promoted violence and hatred from childhood onwards might be part of the painful nation building process and search for ideology, but it certainly fails to instil tolerance and acceptance of plurality under the students' (Malik, 2006: 118). Now if formal state schools are responsible for such unacceptable indoctrination then the argument cannot be used that *madāris* are the seedbeds of terrorism or the 'axes of evil' in South Asia. In fact, it seems as if Islamic extremism has a secularly inspired basis: social conflict, poverty, suppression and state indoctrination—which to my mind, exonerates even a minimalist understanding of Islamic education from instigating people to act radically. Hence, minimalist and maximalist views of Islamic education can barely be traced to the extremist actions of some students in this area, but rather to unfavourable material conditions coupled with state indoctrination.

Islamic thought in Southeast Asia

By far some of the most influential and peaceful Islamic movements in Southeast Asia that overwhelmingly impact the Islamic education in *madāris* of almost more than 230 million Muslims are the Muhammadiyah, Nahdatul Ulama (with a membership of almost 30–40 million, the majority of whom are rural and peasant-based), the Dewan Dakwah Islāmiyah (Indonesian Council for Propagation of the Islamic Faith), the Department of Islamic Development Malaysia (JAKIM), the Institute of Islamic Understanding Malaysia (IKIM), the Angatan Belia Islam Malaisa (Muslim Youth Movements of Malaysia, ABIM), the Majlis Ugama Islām Singapura, and the Islamic Da`wah Council of the Philippines (Yousif, 2006: 454–456). All the aforementioned movements can be classified as advocates for peaceful change in their societies (Yousif, 2006: 462). The Muhammadiyah, the first reformist movement in Indonesia, was founded in 1912 in Yogyakarta, Central Java (Ali, 2005: 5). It is the most respected Islamic educational organisation which serves as a feeder institution for several *madāris* advocating a rational approach to Islamic education. That is, it has adopted a maximalist approach to Islamic education aimed at purifying 'Islamic beliefs and teachings from the practices of animistic values in the Indonesian villages' (Yousif, 2006: 454). This maximalist view of Islamic education is corroborated by the Muhammadiyah's agenda to educate its members to participate in political elections—in other words, its political activities are inseparable from religious life with the aim of cultivating peaceful change (Yousif, 2006: 458).

Moreover, the Nahdatul Ulama ('Revival of Muslim Scholars'), founded in 1926, is the largest Islamic movement in Indonesia and its influence on *madāris* (known as *pesantren*/Islamic boarding schools) is predicated on calls for greater cooperation and understanding among all religious groups in Indonesia, including the support for democratic reform and freedom of expression (Yousif, 2006: 457). To my mind, the educational efforts of Nahdatul Ulama cannot be separated from a maximalist understanding of Islamic education for the reason that the latter is linked to cultivating a moderately religious and political climate in society.

Unlike the aforementioned moderate Islamic movements in Southeast Asia, there are also 'separatist groups' that invariably influence some *madāris* in the region. Motivated by moral frustration, ideological fear of globalisation and Western political and economic hegemony minority groups like Jamāh Islāmiyyah employ violent measures to resolve their problems and gain public attention: 'JI is a radical terrorist Islamic organisation which has emerged as the biggest threat to Southeast Asia security...the JI is part of the globalised *Salafi Jihād* [that is, to establish the Islamic polity through a military takeover of the state] ideology or *Al-Qaedaism*, which was brought to Southeast Asia by Arab migrants from Yemen' (Yousif, 2006: 458–459). They use violence and religious rhetoric through biased interpretations of Islamic texts to advance their cause for an Islamic state. Yet even Jamāh Islāmiyyah and other radical groups like Abū Sayyaf (Bearer of the Sword) in the Philippines, and the militant Pattani United Liberation Organisation in Thailand cannot disagree that Islam does not justify the killing of innocent people. My view is that such organisations violate even a minimalist view of Islamic education with the result that religious leaders are encouraged to play a critical role in directing Muslims towards societal good and to reduce inter-religious conflict (Yousif, 2006: 462). Therefore their reasons for extremist action cannot be inspired by a conception of Islamic education, but rather disgruntledment, ideological inaptitude and political marginalisation. The fact that the Liberal Islam Network (Jaringan Islam Liberal) rose to prominence in Indonesia over the last decade is a vindication that a maximalist view of Islamic education is being aspired to as 'a response to Islamic fundamentalists, who although small in number but great in influence, had adopted an increasingly threatening attitude towards democratic values' (Ali, 2005: 4). The young activists who are members of the Liberal Islam Network 'had been exposed to modern ideas and theories as well as to Islam's traditional sciences, and were familiar with such liberal ideas as freedom of thought, moderation, human rights, democracy, and so forth' (Ali, 2005: 8–9). In a way, this network is sufficient justification that a maximalist view of Islamic education is ubiquitous in the Indonesian Archipelago and that so-called 'fundamentalists constitute a very tiny minority' (Ali, 2005: 9). And, to assert that Southeast Asian *madāris* generally educate people to become extremists would be an unfair assumption. One cannot blame Islam for the rise of Abū Sayyaf, but rather the socio-political conditions in their own countries. Likewise, I cannot imagine condemning Catholicism as being violent in view of terrorism perpetrated in Northern Ireland, neither can one assume that Judaism is responsible for militant Zionism, or public violence be blamed on states for a few movements' acts of terror (such as the Basque separatist movement ETA in Spain, the Direct Action in France, the Red Army in Japan, the Tamil in Sri Lanka, the Sikhs in India, and others elsewhere). Throughout history there have always been links between violence and religion, for instance Christianity and the Crusades, the wars between European kings and Popes, and the bloodshed between Protestants and Catholics in the past (Osman, 2006: 377). What I am suggesting is that Islamic education—whether minimalist or maximalist—in the *madāris* cannot be blamed for the extremist actions of a few.

Islamic education in modern Turkey

The demise of the Ottoman Empire (1299–1918) was followed by the displacement of religion from the actual structure of the state. Since 1923, education in the modern-day Turkish Republic was implemented along a dualist structure: the *medrese* (*madrassah*) being responsible for traditional, religiously situated education, and the *mekteb* (secular school) providing a modernised, reformist education 'aimed at freeing the mind from the dogmatic thinking that [interpretations of] Islam had inculcated in people…[with the goal of] educating new generations of Turks who would think logically' (Heper, 2006: 345). It followed that the founders of the Turkish Republican Party (Cumhuriyet Halk Partisi) in 1923 embarked on a political reform project, known as Kemalism (derived from the name of its founder, Mustafa Kemal Atatürk), and 'closed religious schools, religious courts as well as religious orders, lodges, and shrines' (Heper, 2006: 345).

Through a Directorate of Religious Affairs they appointed prayer leaders and preachers of the mosques and monitored the sermons given at the mosques with the aim of helping to maintain 'an enlightened Islam...[as] a source for noting more than personal ethics' (Heper, 2006: 345). Later advocates of such laicism 'see religion as a barrier to modernisation and regard the medrese and religion itself as a source of ignorance and dogmatism' (Pacaci & Aktay, 2006: 126). In fact, these secularists regarded religion as a personal matter to be separated from matters of the state and religious (Islamic) education as the responsibility of the family.

So, despite the modernisation of Turkey, traditional Islamic education persisted to the extent that many *madāris* were considered as *imam-hatip* schools although they had not been given the same status as lycée/high schools (Pacaci & Aktay, 2006: 127). In such a way, Islamic education was confined to the 'realm of the private' (Pacaci & Aktay, 2006: 128). Currently there are about 23 faculties of Ilāhiyāt (religious education) in universities that mostly attract students from the *imam-hatip* schools (*madāris*) (Pacaci & Aktay, 2006: 128). I am particularly interested in the rationale which seems to inform these *imam-hatip* schools in modern Turkey. It is widely acknowledged that a graduate from an *imam-hatip* school can join a faculty of Ilāhiyāt at one of the universities with the intention to be trained as a person who not only depends on the Qurān as the most basic source of religion, but also is capable of evaluating Turkish cultural heritage and producing solutions to problems faced. Such a student will be further exposed to an education aimed at providing students with knowledge of religious sciences, culture and history. Many graduates from universities in fact go on to teach in *imam-hatip* schools (*madāris*) (Pacaci & Aktay, 2006: 139), which emphasises that integrated courses of religious culture and modernised knowledge are not considered to be harmful to a person's education. The state has increasingly acknowledged the need for Islamic education to be taught along the lines of 'Islam's espousal of tolerance' (Pacaci & Aktay, 2006: 140). In my view, a maximalist view of Islamic education is not distant from the *imam-hatip* schools (*madāris*) for the reason that these institutions are also considered to be important for secularist Turkey in producing 'pious people whose moral qualities such as industriousness, just behaviour, respect for the people, tolerance for rivals, and search for peace and harmony in the community and society would inevitably reflect upon their politics' (Heper, 2006: 348). Likewise, the fact that most of these schools are still under the control of the state suggests that the current ruling party's (Adalet ve Kalkinma Partisi, AKP or the Justice and Development Party) advocacy for conservative democracy, taking a stand against fundamentalism through emphasising harmony and dialogue, and serving as a bridge between civilisations has the same possibility of manifesting in their educational programmes. In this way, a maximalist view of Islamic education cannot be distanced from *imam-hatip* schools (*madāris*) in modern Turkey.

I shall now extensively examine Islamic education in South Africa, focusing primarily on practices in some *madāris* (Muslim afternoon schools; usually from 15:00 to 17:00). As has been mentioned earlier, *madāris* are different from Muslim private schools (about 75 in the country at the time of writing this book). Muslim private schools mostly follow a state-prescribed curriculum intertwined with an Islamic studies programme. These schools are autonomous and receive some support from the state for their day-to-day operations. The afternoon *madrassah* is my focus of investigation for three reasons: firstly, it has retained the name *madrassah*, unlike the existing Muslim private schools or seminaries, and consequently I want to show that understanding these *madāris* primarily involves uncovering minimalist and maximalist meanings that constitute their activities; secondly, Muslim private schools have a greater state influence in terms of prescribed curricula and the country's new outcomes-based education system; and thirdly, my argument against extremism is connected to the practices of *madāris* which have been accused of by many as being responsible for terrorist activities—in fact the very term '*madrassah*' nowadays carries a negative connotation.

Islamic education in South African *madāris*

A large number of the early Muslim immigrants and slaves were from orthodox Muslim strongholds such as Coromandel, Bengal and to a lesser extent Malabar in India (Bradlow & Cairns, 1978: 103). However, the first recorded arrival of free Muslims, namely the Mardyckers from Amboyna—an Indonesian Island—was in 1658 (Mahida, 1993: 2). According to Da Costa (1990: 30), the early Muslims came primarily from India (36,4%), the East Indies (31,47%), Africa (26,65%), Ceylon (3,1%, now Sri Lanka), Malaya (0,49%), Mauritius (0,18%) and 0,4% from elsewhere, whereas

1,31% of the slaves were unidentified. Now, despite the fact that the dominant jurisprudential school of thought (*madhab*) in India was *Hanafism*, this excluded the Malabar Coast—from which, as stated above, most of the early Muslims came where *Shafi`ism* was dominant (Da Costa, 1990: 51). Hence, it can be claimed that during the 17th and 18th centuries the majority of the early Muslims were *Shafi`is* (Da Costa, 1990: 30). This is so, considering the fact that both the East Indies islands and East Africa were also *Shafi`i* strongholds (Da Costa, 1990: 51–51). Of course, this does not mean that there were no *Hanafi* adherents during the first two centuries of Islam at the Cape. But, during this period, 'Cape Muslims were almost exclusively *Shafi`is*' (Davids, 1994a: 82).

During the first two centuries of Islam at the Cape, *tasawwuf* as well as an aberration of it in the form of mystical Sufi practices constituted Islamic education in *madāris* (Davids, 1994: 47). Tayob (1995: 54) claims that '(u)ntil 1804, the resources of a mystical Islam provided spiritual support [for Muslims] under conditions of slavery'. Moreover, Da Costa (1994a: 129) claims that 'special orders of mysticism' shaped Muslim practices between the 17th and 19th centuries as a consequence of European colonialism in Africa and Asia at the time. Hence, during the early years of Islam at the Cape, Islamic education was intertwined with mysticism which in a way shaped the concept in a minimalist sense for the reason that such mystical orders were mostly associated with degrees of passiveness.

With these *tasawwuf* and mystical orientations, the early Cape Muslims, despite being prohibited from openly practising Islam, are said to have provided the 'framework in which such people as Tuan Guru [Muslim leader at the Cape] could work' (Bradlow & Cairns, 1978: 2, 106). What this means is that before the arrival of Tuan Guru at the Cape in 1780, Muslims in 1667—prohibited from practising Islam in public—already practised *tasawwuf* which could have been from the *Qādiriyyah* order (Da Costa, 1994: 130). *Tasawwuf* orders like these constitute units of 'socio-religious interaction', whereby 'inside these *sufi* orders groups gather around a master of spiritual guidance (*murshid*) seeking training through association or companionship…The disciples are linked by common devotions and spiritual discipline within these structures…being bound by sacred obligations, form a holy family' (Da Costa, 1994: 60–61)—practices which to my mind enhance the moral consciousness of people perhaps in a minimalist way.

The first prominent exile among the early Muslim religious leaders was Shaykh Yusuf of Macassar, banished to the Cape in 1694. He is claimed to have been the first *murshid* (*tasawwuf* guide) who introduced the Khalwātiyyah Sufi order—which has its origins in 14th century Turkey—to the Cape (Da Costa, 1992: 11). Moreover, according to Da Costa (1990: 61), *tasawwuf* activities include 'communal religious practices on the first, third, seventh, fortieth nights succeeding a [Muslim] funeral', the celebration of the Prophet's birthday (Maulūd al-Nabi), a common Qādiriyyah practice, *Rātib al-Haddad,* which involves readings from the Qurān, recitations in praise of Allāh and the offering of supplications and prayers (Davids, 1980: 95). In addition, these *tasawwuf* practices were dominated by *dhikr,* literally the remembrance of Allāh. It has become synonymous with verbal (single or communal) utterances in the forms of *du`ā* (supplications and confessions addressed to Allāh) and *salawāt* (invocations of the blessings bestowed on Prophet Muhammad (SAW) and his followers).[2]

Undoubtedly, the *tasawwuf* tradition established by the early Cape Muslim *tuans* (*tasawwuf* masters) made an indelible impact on the practices of Muslims, in particular in the Cape. This influence and diffusion of *tasawwuf* can be seen from the activities associated with the Khalwātiyyah order and which are still widely practised in the Cape today. As stated by Da Costa (1994: 31), these activities include 'recital of sections of the Qurān and certain litanies, either at the grave or at the previous residence of the deceased…The ceremony has different names: an *arwāh* (the plural of *rūh* which is the Arabic for soul), a '*werk*' (the Afrikaans for 'work' which is a translation of the Arabic `*aml*), and *hājah* (the Arabic for a 'necessity'…The use of this ceremony has today been extended, and it is not uncommon for a *hājah* to be given or held (as the expression goes) on birthdays, anniversaries, before a naming ceremony, or on any other auspicious occasion. It is also quite common for it to be incorporated into other religious ceremonies, such as *Maulūd al-Nabi.'*

Did some of these *tasawwuf* practices influence Islamic education in *madāris?* The Habibiyah Mosque and Madrassah complex in the Cape, for example, consisting of a number of educational institutions such as *madāris,* is renowned for its practising of the Chistiyyah[3] *tasawwuf* rituals (Da Costa, 1994b: 137), which suggests that *tassawwuf* have been practised in the *madāris.* Of course, learners at *madāris* who are socialised with the *tasawwuf* epic poems (*riwāyāt*) and *salawāt* (invocations recited on the Prophet Muhammad (SAW)) have to rely overwhelmingly on memorisation. And, it happens to be that many *madrassah* teachers, as well as learners, successfully and impressively memorise several *tasawwuf* litanies. Da Costa (1994: 112–113) mentions the *tasawwuf* practices of learners of the late Shaykh Muhammad Sālih Hendricks (whom he initiated into the Alawiyyah Sufi[4] order) commonly known as Zāwiyyah *murids* who 'came to play prominent roles in the religious affairs of Muslims (which include *madāris*)'. Moreover, with specific reference to the impact of *tasawwuf* on *madāris*, Davids (1994: 55) mentions the memorisation of twenty attributes of Allāh (known as 'the twintagh siefaats') or the Sanūsiyyah, formulated by the Sanūsiyyah (*tasawwuf*) order and which 'remained to be the main teaching subject of the *madāris* of Cape Town until well into the 1950s and 1960s'. What seems evident from an emphasis on memorising the *tasawwuf* litanies is the fact that understanding has not always been encouraged—thus pointing to a minimalist view of Islamic education. Davids (1994: 55) himself claims that as a child he was expected to memorise the concepts of the Sanūsiyyah 'without fully comprehending them'. For this reason it can be claimed that a particular understanding of *tasawwuf* on the part of many of its adherents opened up the possibility for rote learning and hence, a minimalist understanding of Islamic education, more specifically *ta`līm* (instruction).

Furthermore, regarding mysticism, Tayob (1995: 42) explains that it 'reached its apogee' with the arrival of Tuan Guru. Imam Abdullah Ibn Qādi Abdu al-Salām, known as Tuan Guru, was a prince from Tidore in the Ternate Islands of Indonesia (Mahida, 1993: 8). While imprisoned on Robben Island, he wrote several copies of the Qurān from memory. He also wrote a book on Islamic jurisprudence and theology, based on Shafi`ite principles (Chohan, 1988: 68–69). This book of his, Ma`rifah al-Islām wa al-Imān (Manifestations of Islam and Faith), in the words of Davids, 'deals exclusively with the concepts of belief (*aqīdah*) and as such deals with that part of the *Sharī`ah* (Islamic law) known as `*ilm al-kalām*, that is, the principles of belief or the knowledge of the existence of God—the *Sharī`ah* being divided into two distinct parts, the `*ilm al-kalām* and *fiqh*—the latter being concerned with the practices of the religion, governing its rules and regulations, and hence projected as Islamic jurisprudence' (Davids, 1994: 55). Moreover, the Shāfi`i-dominated era of Tuan Guru was also characterised by the esoteric practice of writing talismans (*azīmats*) and remedies (*ishārah*) for 'psychological and physical cures' (Tayob, 1995: 42). In this way, in the wake of slavery and political domination, the early Cape Muslims submitted themselves willingly and unquestioningly to the authority of the *tuan*[5] or *shaykh*[6] who, they believed, protected them against the inhuman and unjust laws perpetrated by the state. This very practice of mystical Islam constituted the possibility of accepting, without understanding and questioning, the supremacy of the *tuan* as the sole protector of Muslims. In other words, it opened up the possibility for a conformist pattern of Muslim behaviour mostly associated with a minimalist understanding of Islamic education. This does not mean that conformity in an intolerant religious environment (which was the case in the 17th and 18th centuries of Muslim settlement at the Cape) was problematic. But, when the socio-political conditions have changed, then this kind of esoteric conformity to the *tuan* or *shaykh* has the potential to elicit uncritical and conditioned behaviour on the part of Muslims, which confirms a minimalist understanding of Islamic education. Mystical orientations such as the above-mentioned practices were later supplemented by *madāris*. On being released from prison, Tuan Guru established the first *madrassah* at the Cape in Dorp Street (Cape Town) in 1793 (Mahida, 1993: 9). At this school, learners were taught precepts from the Qurān and to read and write the Arabic language, as well as to study his Shāfi'i treatise, *Ma`rifah al-Islām wal-Imān* (Mahida, 1993: 9). Hence, Shāfi'ism became the dominant school of Islamic thought that influenced the practices and institutions of the early Muslims.

At the end of the 19th and the beginning of the 20th centuries there was a large influx of both Hanafis and Shāfi'is in South Africa. But at the Cape, the Hanafis continued to remain a minority (Davids, 1994: 76). In fact, 90% of the Cape Muslims at that time were Shāfi'is (Davids, 1980: 52). Da Costa's (1990: 225) research on schools of thought at the Cape today, whereby it was found that the Muslim community comprises 80,5% Shāfi'is and 16,8% Hanafis, also vindicates this point. The present Hanafi jurisprudential school of thought prevails largely among the Indian Muslims (Da Costa, 1990: 357). Nevertheless, as early as the 1860s, one sees the influence of Hanafi thought on *madāris*, with the arrival of Abubakr Effendi (Turkish-Kurdish scholar) at the Cape on the request of the British government. One of his main tasks was to resolve the disputes about successorship at Cape mosques and to guide and instruct Muslims in

Islamic law (*shari'ah*). His book the *Bayān al-Dīn* (the explanation of religion)—a Hanafi treatise on Islam—became the textbook implemented at the school of higher Islamic theology established by him. This text was written in Arabic-Afrikaans, that is, Arabic script with Afrikaans sounds. On several occasions Effendi was summoned to testify in the Cape Supreme Court to resolve the issue about the mosque disputes. According to Davids (1980), it was Effendi's views on the Friday congregational prayers that started the Hanafi-Shāfi'i controversy. For example, according to the Shāfi'i school, forty worshippers had to be present in mosque on a Friday if the Friday congregational prayers (*jumua'h* prayers) were to be offered. On the contrary, the Hanafi school was of the opinion that congregational prayers could be offered if three worshippers were present and unlike the Shāfi'is would not offer the usual mid-afternoon prayers.[7] The reluctance on the part of both the Shāfi'i and the Hanafi religious leaders to engage with different points of view about issues involving Islamic law, gave rise to perennial disagreements between Shafi'i and Hanafi Muslims. Although Effendi's students were drawn mainly from prominent Shāfi'i Cape Muslims, which included the three grandsons of Tuan Guru, his unpopular pronouncements such as declaring crayfish and snoek forbidden (*harām*) for consumption, infuriated the majority of Shāfi'i Muslims (Davids, 1980: 54). Despite the opposition Effendi received from the majority of the Shāfi'i Muslims, his Hanafi teachings had some impact (although minimal) on early Muslim practices, as can be seen from the establishment of the first Hanafi mosque in 1881 (Mahida, 1993: 32). In essence, the dominant *madhab* (jurisprudential school of thought) at the Cape was (and remains) Shāfi'ism.

Shāfi'ism and Hanafism did not remain confined to the Cape. In 1840 there were 150 Muslims in the Eastern Cape town of Port Elizabeth. In 1860, the first indentured Muslims of whom between seven and ten per cent were Muslims (Tayob, 1995: 55) arrived in Natal from India (Mahida, 1993: 18, 23). In 1871 the second group of Indians, of whom 80% were Muslims (known as the 'passenger' Indians because they paid their own fares to South Africa) arrived (Tayob, 1995; 55). Although some of these Muslims were traders, the majority came primarily from the rural areas of Gujarat in India, which, unlike the Malabar Coast as mentioned earlier, was Hanafi-dominated. These previously indentured and 'passenger' Indians (including Muslims) settled in three main provinces at that time, namely

Natal (KwaZulu-Natal), Transvaal (Gauteng) and the Cape (Western Cape). The Hanafi Indian Muslims at the Cape built their first mosque (Quwwat al-Islām) in 1892 (Tayob, 1995: 57). The second group of Hanafi-orientated Indian Muslims came mostly from the Kokanee-speaking Bombay Presidency in India. Aspects of *tasawwuf* in the form of Qādiriyyah and Chistiyyah orders were also practised by them. In Transvaal (Gauteng) and Natal (KwaZulu-Natal) Hanafi-dominated mosque committees (comprising prominent and wealthy Muslim individuals) dominated *madāris* (Tayob, 1995: 55–57). The religious leaders and teachers who served these institutions either came from India or had been trained in an institution in South Asia. Tayob (1995: 63) argues that they established associations (*jāmi'āts*) through which they attempted to assert their authority by introducing theological and juridical directives in the community. They defined Islam and thereby determined the elements of Islamic orthodoxy and orthopraxy within the institutions. In 1922 the Jāmi'atul 'Ulamā Transvaal (primarily following Deoband teachings) was founded with the aim also of promoting, developing and unifying the Islamic educational system in South Africa (Mahida, 1993: 57). Subsequently, the Jāmi'at's Islamic educational activities, mostly based on Hanafi principles, included the affiliation of various *madāris* of the Gauteng to the Jāmi'āt in 1964 (Haron, 1988: 45, 57). In the 1990s, the Jāmi'āt supervised in excess of seventy *madāris* in Gauteng (Mahida, 1993: 57). Moreover, the Jāmi'atul 'Ulamā Transvaal (Gauteng) recognised the limitations of numerous ill-qualified imams [religious leaders] and teachers it comprised and, with the support of the wealthy Mia family, established the Waterval Islamic Institute (Gauteng) in 1940 (Tayob, 1995: 66). In 1952 the Jāmi'atul 'Ulamā Natal (KwaZulu-Natal), with mostly Deoband religious leaders, was founded to guide the Muslims, and to supervise *madāris* and provide syllabi (Mahida, 1993: 70; Tayob, 1995: 70). According to Tayob (1995: 70), 'they built their base in the province on support from the Tablighi Jamaat, a *madrasah* network consisting of teachers, a syllabus, and an alliance with some powerful business leaders'. So, it seems as if Islamic education in KwaZulu-Natal *madāris* was shaped by minimalist views of Islamic education, considering that the Deoband and Tabligh Jamaat's orientation was dictated to by a moral and passive religious adherence to the primary sources of Islam.

In 1952 the Central Islamic Trust was founded in Johannesburg to promote Islamic education (Mahida, 1993: 75). Other institutions which were established to advance Islamic education include the Orient Islamic State-Aided School, Durban (1959), the Lenasia Muslim Association (1962), the Boorhanol Recreation Movement, Cape Town (1966), the Cape Muslim Assembly (1967), the Majlis al-Shūra al-Islām, Cape (1968), the Islamic Educational and Religious Trust, Durban (1970), the Institute of Islamic Shari`ah Studies, Cape (1972), the Darul `Ulum Newcastle (1973) and the Sunni Jāmi`atul `Ulamā of South Africa—formed by newly qualified religious leaders from India and Pakistan in 1978 (Mahida, 1993: 87–114). This Jami`at is a splinter group of the Jāmi`atul `Ulamā (KwaZulu-Natal) and clearly articulates anti-Deoband sentiments. They are also commonly known as the Barelwis. In fact, the Sunni Jāmi`atul `Ulamā perpetuate a kind of mystical Islam closely linked to the *tasawwuf* practices established by two renowned Sufi saints buried in Durban (KwaZulu-Natal). The first Sufi master, Shaykh Ahmad—known as Majzoob Badsha Peer (enraptured saintly saint)—who died in 1886 is said to 'have exuded prodigious and mysterious charisma and power' (Tayob, 1995: 71). The second Sufi master, Shah Ghulam Muhammad Soofi Siddiqi (commonly known as Soofi Saheb), who belonged to the Chistiyyah Sufi order, arrived in KwaZulu-Natal in 1895. The *tasawwuf* practices introduced by him, such as the celebration of the anniversary of Badsha Peer, the commemoration of the martyrdom of Husayn (the Prophet's grandson), the condolence procession during the first ten days of Muharram (the first month of the Islamic calendar) and *maulūd al-nabi* (the Prophet's birthday), greatly influenced the practices in the *madāris*, mosques and orphanages he established (Tayob, 1995: 72). To my mind, these practices, coupled with the political order of apartheid at the time, enhanced a minimalist approach to Islamic education, as these organisations that controlled *madāris* did not always encourage Muslims to challenge the state. They rather urged them to appeal privately to Allāh to improve their religious consciousness and perseverance during times of political turmoil in the country.

Regarding the development of Shāfi`i and Hanafi institutions in South Africa, Mahida (1993: 114–146) notes that the Madrasah Arabia Islamia, Azadville (1982), the Darul-`Ulum Aleemia Razvia (following the Barelwi trend), Chatsworth (1983), the Darul-`Ulum Zakariyah, Johannesburg (1983), the Habibiyah Islamic College, Cape Town (1984), the Islamic

Educational Organisation of Southern Africa, Durban (1985), the Lenasia Muslim School (1986) and the Islamic College of South Africa (1990) were established. The Islamic College of South Africa amalgamated about five years ago with the Muslim Judicial Council's Dār al-Arqām to form the Islamic Peace University of Southern Africa. Hence, it is clear from the number of institutions that Islamic education has flourished since the early days of Muslim settlement in South Africa. It is significant that the Western Cape institutions mostly use the Shafi`i teachings, whereas the Gauteng and KwaZulu-Natal institutions adhere mostly to Hanafi teachings that are related to either a Deoband or a Barelwi perspective.

From the history of the development of Islamic institutions in South Africa it is evident that no formal Wahhabi institution has been established. However, this does not mean that some South African religious leaders who studied in Saudi Arabia (especially during the second half of this century) were not perhaps influenced by Wahhabi thought. Da Costa (1994: 137) claims that 'almost all the shaykhs and imams in the Cape Peninsula who had studied overseas [in particular in Makkah] during the first half of this century and before [such as Shaykh Ahmad Behardien (d.1973), Muhammad Tayb Jassiem (d.1972), Abdullah Jamal al-Din (d. 1948) and Imam Abd al-Basir (d. 1962)], were well known in the community for the exercise of many *tasawwuf* practices. All of these shaykhs and imams also celebrated the night of the middle of the month of Sha`ban (called Nisfu-Sha`ban with the reciting of the Yāsin—one of the chapters of the Qurān) three times accompanied by special applications. The common name for this night is Ruwah'—a practice very much in vogue in *madāris* and the broader Muslim community today. By implication, some of the religious leaders and Muslim *madrassah* teachers who studied in Makkah during the second half of 20th century could have been influenced, to some extent, by Wahhabi thought (in particular the Wahhabis' suppression of popular Sufism). This claim is vindicated by the fact that shaykhs, for example, Shaykh Abu Bakr Najjaar (who also studied in Makkah) opposed the *tasawwuf* perspective enunciated by Maulana Khuster in 1970 (Da Costa, 1994: 138). The Wahhabi influence has been viewed with some circumspection by Muslims, as demonstrated by the accusation waged by Barelwis in KwaZulu-Natal against the Deoband-Tabligh alliance[8] for advocating Wahhabi beliefs which were associated with practices of reform (Cilliers, 1983: 126). However, this does not mean that Wahhabism flourished in South Africa. Clearly, a number of community structures directly associated with the *tasawwuf* tradition have remained dominant in the Western Cape (Da Costa, 1994: 141). Hence it is my understanding that the *tasawwuf* perspective, rather than Wahhabi thought, dominates many institutions, including *madāris* in the Western Cape. And, considering that *tasawwuf* as practised in South Africa can be linked to passive, non-violent and peaceful religious practices, it would not be an exaggeration to claim that a minimalist view of Islamic education was operative in several *madāris*. In essence, one can effectively claim that three trends dominate *madāris*, namely Shāfi'ism, Deobandism and Barelwism (the latter two groups are predominantly followers of Hanafism). Moreover, many *madāris* are also shaped by the practices of *tasawwuf*, characteristic of both Shafi'ism and Hanafism. It can be assumed that one of the reasons as to why no apparent Wahhabi institution has been established at the Cape is that many of the Cape religious leaders who studied in Makkah were steeped in the practices of *tasawwuf*. For example, the Makkan tutors of Shaykh Muhammad Salih Hendricks (d.1945) who, according to Da Costa (1994b: 106, 193), is 'one of the rare Islamic scholars in South Africa' were prominent *tasawwuf* masters. And, considering that at times intolerant Wahhabism did not find pedagogical spaces in most *madāris*, the possibility for violent Islamic discourses were highly unlikely within a minimalist framework of Islamic education.

I shall now further explore what I consider to be the practice of minimalist Islamic education in some South African *madāris*. According to Nadvi, in KwaZulu-Natal and Gauteng, the four major Muslim seminaries (Dārul 'Ulūms)—the Azadville, the Zakariya Madrassah and the Waterval Islamic Institute in Gauteng, and the Dārul 'Ulūm Newcastle in KwaZulu-Natal follow traditional systems that only stress a conformist adherence to revealed knowledge as isolated from non-revealed sciences. Affiliated to these institutions are several *madāris* which, like their feeder institutions, are 'rigid' and 'unwilling to accept change' towards the modernisation of Islamic education (Nadvi, 1988: 55). This means that the controlling religious leaders of the aforementioned *madāris* seem to be reluctant to introduce new ideas. It is my contention that their conformist dispositions have paved the way for a minimalist view of Islamic education in *madāris*. For Nadvi (1988: 56), *madāris* 'are dichotomised and sandwiched between the two forces, the retrogressive and the progressive...to some 'Ulama [or religious leaders, Islamic] education means merely the religious education (Dīni ta`līm) and not the...(natural sciences)'. Once again, these religious leaders seem to bifurcate Islamic education into 'revealed knowledge' and 'non-revealed sciences', and hence it can be argued that they encourage a minimalist approach to Islamic education. Moreover, Nadvi (1988: 59) claims that 'progressive' centres, which control many madāris and mosques, include the Orient Islamic Educational Institute (KwaZulu-Natal), the Central Islamic Trust (Gauteng), the Lenasian Muslim Association and the Nūr al-Islam Centre (Gauteng), whereas 'retrogressive' and 'passionately progressive' centres include the Jāmi`atul `Ulamā and the Benoni Muslim Jamāt (Gauteng).

Now that I have given an account of minimalist understandings of Islamic education in some madāris in South Africa prior to the 1990s (including the apartheid era), I want to ascertain which features of Islamic education further enhanced such minimalist views, with reference to Islamic education in the 1990s and 2000s. In fact, with reference to an empirical project I embarked upon recently, I wish to argue that Islamic education in madāris seems to be functioning on a minimalist-maximalist continuum with some bias towards maximalism at times.

Minimalist-maximalist views of Islamic education in contemporary (1990–2010) South African madāris: The apartheid and post-apartheid periods

Thus far I have shown how, before 1990, the great majority of madāris in South Africa came to be associated with the teaching of minimalist understandings of Islamic education. Such understandings of Islamic education were shaped mainly by many conformist religious leaders and teachers, especially against the background of the political hegemony of apartheid that curtailed the aspirations of several Muslim leaders for a just socio-political dispensation. Of course many views have been expressed about the apparent complacency of several Muslim religious leaders during the apartheid era, especially about their unwillingness to support societal change openly. To my mind such claims can be linked to the passivity of several Muslim leaders, considering their minimalist understanding that Islam demands adherence to the laws of the state, albeit unjust at the time. However, other more progressive Muslim religious leaders, of whom some were incarcerated for their opposition to apartheid, openly supported the anti-apartheid liberation movement and also influenced the thinking about Islamic education in a maximalist way.

Before showing how minimalist views of Islamic education unfolded in *madāris* I shall briefly examine some of the views of prominent Muslim religious leaders and teachers with the aim of showing that their views cannot be exclusively linked to extremism and hence, violent action. In the late 1980s Moosa (1989: 80) identified certain conformist attitudes amongst many religious leaders: 'There is no perceivable gap between their conservative views and that of the religious constituencies [Islamic institutions] they serve.' This finding is supported by Rehman (1988: 50), who claims that in KwaZulu-Natal, for example, *maulānas* (religious scholars or graduates of an Islamic seminar in South Asia) of the Sunni Jāmi`atul `Ulamā of South Africa prepared and implemented syllabi 'in all the affiliated Madressas'. Firstly, according to Moosa (1989: 73), 'rigid conservatism' is articulated by religious groups, represented by the Muslim Judicial Council (MJC), the Jāmi`atul `Ulamā (Council of Theologians) of Transvaal (Gauteng), the Jāmi`atul `Ulamā of Natal (KwaZulu-Natal) and the Majlis al-`Ulama of South Africa. In his view, these religious leaders' 'tradition…[is] static and conservative', characterised by what he refers to as 'certain ambiguous and conservative tendencies' (Moosa, 1989: 74). He cites the example of Muslim religious leaders who, during the apartheid era, encouraged Muslims to conform to state rule, for the reason that the government allowed Muslims to pray, build mosques and perform pilgrimage (Moosa, 1989: 75–76). In his view, the religious leaders are intent on preserving 'pre-modern religious discourse, especially its order and authority structures…[which] takes precedence over creative thinking and the adaptation of Islam to modern circumstances' (Moosa, 1989: 81). These conformist religious leaders perpetuate a notion of Islam in the *madāris* 'which is captive to an unchanging symbolic…which fosters preservation by resisting change'. To my mind, such a conformist attitude towards Islamic education clearly confirms a minimalist stance. Secondly, Naude (1982: 34) also recognises the conformist attitudes of the Jāmi`atul `Ulamā in Transvaal (Gauteng), who in general 'see their task, however, as the age-old traditional role of reiterating Islam's truths. They alone have the authority to do so and in that capacity they will not be bullied by modernists.' Thus, it is seems plausible to argue that religious authorities in the country advocate a minimalist view of Islamic education by not necessarily allowing for flexibility in Islamic thought—a claim vindicated by the Jāmi`atul `Ulamā's satisfaction with the status quo 'as long as they can carry out their Islamic work [leading prayers, rendering sermons, conducting marriages and burials, and so on] undisturbed' (Naude, 1982: 35–38)—a position which clearly reflects a minimalist understanding of Islamic education. Moreover, their 'doctrine of obedience' whereby Muslims were urged to conform to an 'unjust ruler' during the apartheid era vindicates their conformist attitudes which they considered as 'better than anarchy'. It is this conformist attitude which not only expressed their minimalist stance on Islamic education but also made them less vulnerable to extremist, violent action. Thirdly, Lubbe (1989: 79) identifies a 'rift' which appeared and 'has not completely healed' between religious leaders of the Muslim Judicial Council (MJC) and intellectuals of the Muslim Assembly (an established Islamic institution). Now, despite the fact that the MJC has 'competent scholars who are doing good work in the area of Islamic jurisprudence' (Lubbe, 1989: 79–82), they do not have an 'impressive track record regarding unity in the Cape Muslim community' and, can it be said that the MJC cannot be exonerated from being conformist, which is evident from its unwillingness to engage (so it seems) with changing views of other 'intellectuals'. Lubbe (1989: 79) sums up the conformist views of the MJC as follows: 'The accumulation of power by the MJC and its unwillingness to share it, stood diametrically opposed to its ability to unite people and to keep them united. In the final analysis then, the MJC will have to take the greater part of the blame that Muslim unity remains an elusive ideal.' What follows from this, is that because of the MJC's seeming 'unwillingness' to engage with others and to give some consideration to contending viewpoints of others who 'tried to enforce a modern understanding of Islam' (Tayob, 1995: 49) it can argued that the organisation is intent on articulating a minimalist view of Islamic education for the reason that a lack of engagement with contending views precludes any claim to a maximalist view of Islamic education. In seems as if the aforementioned minimalist stances on Islamic education filtered through to many *madāris* during the apartheid years. Before moving on to a discussion of Islamic education as it existed during the post-apartheid years in South Africa, I shall firstly examine the minimalist views of Islamic education which seem to have dominated the pre-apartheid period.

Throughout Islam's history in South Africa rote learning seems to have been a dominant practice in *madāris*. During the early days of Muslim settlement at the Cape (18th and 19th centuries), 'rote-learning and communal recitation [traditional methods] were used in the instruction of religious knowledge to the children' (Chohan, 1988: 68). It is understandable that rote learning during these early years of Muslim settlement at the Cape was associated with theology, law, jurisprudence and *tasawwuf*, for the reason that the early Muslim slaves and converts (subordinates of colonial slavery) were victims of conformity, caused by colonial domination. Rote learning merely emphasises the importance of conformity, that is, memorising lots of religious knowledge without questioning. In the early 1990s (the apartheid period), in a report about a case study of *madāris* received by the Boorhanul Recreation Movement, a community-service organisation in the Bo-Kaap, Ajam (1990: 91) found that 'the traditional *madrassah* teaching context [that of the early Shafi'i *madāris*] in which they [teachers] had been socialised', was recreated by them. This means that rote learning continued to dominate Islamic education in *madāris*, despite the oppressive socio-historical climate in the country. Of course, change is not necessarily a good thing in itself. But, when our thinking becomes disconnected from the actual context in which we live, then there is a particular problem. This is a pertinent matter in this context, especially bearing in mind that institutionalised state repression was at its zenith. Also, change can occur in two different areas: firstly, we can change our thinking to adapt to our changing circumstances, and secondly, we can change our circumstances so as to bring them in line with our thinking. It is precisely these stifling and inflexible attitudes on the part of proponents of Islamic education in *madāris* (as shown in the report during the apartheid years) who preferred not to adapt their practices to changing times that accentuates their unstated support for a minimalist view of Islamic education. This is worth noting if one considers that some of the leading figures in the Western Cape had either been students in Makkah or at Al-Azhar (Egypt), or were in contact with those who had studied in Makkah or at Al-Azhar, of whom some were reluctant to introduce change. Haron (1988: 53) claimed that Muslim seminaries in the Western Cape, such as Usūl al-Dīn and the Islamic Institute, are headed by theologians trained in Egypt and Saudi Arabia. These seminaries 'produce a number of local theologians [including Islamic teachers] who have been employed by the Madaris'. Now it appears as if these Islamic teachers lay too much emphasis on the acquisition of knowledge, neglecting creativity. That is, they remain conformist. This claim is ratified by Ajam (1990: 91), who argues that most Muslim teachers in *madāris* in the Western Cape lacked 'imagination' and 'orientation'. Consequently, one finds that the techniques used by these Muslim teachers during the apartheid years continued into the next century (as I shall show later on). These techniques include rote learning and parrot-like memorisation of Islamic precepts and Qurānic verses.[9] This means that emphasis is placed on the recitation and memorisation (*hifz*) of the Qurān. In fact, learners' progress at many contemporary *madāris* is still assessed in terms of their ability to recite the Qurān in a melodious style (known in the oral tradition as *lagu*) and in their prowess in narrating Ahādith. Moreover, rote learning which, in the words of Davids (1994: 55), requires of one 'to memorise [Islamic] concepts...without fully comprehending them' is very prevalent in the Western Cape. Of course, the memorisation of the Qurān in itself is not a problem. In the Western Cape, several *huffāz* (those who have memorised the entire Qurān) have always performed significant 'socio-religious functions in the Muslim community, such as leading the obligatory prayers (especially the *tarāwih* or prayers during Ramadān—Islamic month of fasting), reciting at weddings, marriage ceremonies, and fund-raising activities' (Da Costab, 1994: 126). These *huffāz* enjoyed 'a special status in the community, and they are looked upon with considerable admiration, and even awe'. The title of *hāfiz*, which the community bestows on them because they have memorised the Qurān, further strengthens this status (Da Costa, 1994b: 126). However, in many *madāris* there is still an emphasis on memorisation only, without understanding. This demonstrates a minimalist understanding of Islamic education, especially considering that several *huffāz* do not understand classical Arabic (Da Costa, 1994b: 127). In addition, as pointed out by Da Costa (1994b: 136–137), many of the *huffāz* taught their students *tasawwuf* recitals such as the litanies and epic poems (*riwāyāt*) in *Maulūd Barzanji Nazm* (an epic poem dealing with aspects of the birth and life of the Prophet Muhammad (SAW), *Rātib al-Haddad* and *Rātib al-Attas* (both constitute a combination of litanies and invocations generally recited in the Alawiyyah order). These litanies and epic poems (as well as the Qurān) were often memorised by students without understanding. This did not impede the growth and widespread practice of *tasawwuf* recitals on the part of Muslims. In my view, it encouraged rote learning in *madāris*, for the reason that many of the *tasawwuf* proponents, like the *huffāz*, became *madrassah* teachers. An emphasis on rote learning and memorisation only constitute a minimalist understanding of Islamic education for the reason that Islamic education covers socialisation, understanding, questioning, challenging and connecting education to the relevant socio-political context. Moreover, the Boorhanul Recreation Movement's report on *madāris* confirms that a maximalist understanding of Islamic education was actively discouraged by most Muslim teachers, who lacked 'the ability to make the educational content come alive' (Ajam, 1990: 91). As noted by Abdullah (1982: 125), a maximalist view of Islamic education cannot be restricted to rote learning: 'Besides helping the students acquire the facts and the mental skills, Islamic education aims at encouraging sound thinking…[a] deep understanding and not mere rote-learning.' Wan Daud (1990: 108) asserts that 'memorization without understanding is mechanical, uncreative and inert'—that is, tantamount to a minimalist view of Islamic education. Similarly, the conditions in *madāris* during the apartheid period are distinctly different from those in which the early *madāris* emerged. To recreate the traditional method, concentrating on rote learning and memorisation only, would be to ignore perpetual, historical, temporal and societal changes that influence the thoughts, ideas and understandings of people. Once again, it seems as if the reluctance of the *madrassah* leaders to initiate change during the apartheid period points towards the dominance of a minimalist understanding of Islamic education at that time.

Further evidence of the dominance of a minimalist understanding of Islamic education in South African *madāris* throughout the early 1990s (pre-democratic period), is shown by the fact that most of these schools were conducted according to the volition of often unqualified teachers (Chohan, 1988: 68; Haron, 1988: 44–45; Lubbe, 1989: 66) who were reasonably acquainted with Qurānic recitation and discouraged questioning since they lacked imagination (Ajam, 1990: 90). These *madāris* also lacked a coordinated, intersubjective Islamic education system despite modest efforts by Majlis al-Shura (est. 1968), the Al-Jāmi`a Co-ordinating Council of Madaris (est. 1981), and the modernisation efforts of the then Islamic College of Southern Africa (which later became the International Peace University of Southern Africa) (Haron, 1988: 45). A lack of integrated curricula between the rational and revealed sciences, as well as several institutions' aversion to progressive ideas (Nadvi, 1988: 61) confirms that minimalist views on Islamic education were ubiquitous in *madāris* during the pre-democratic period in South Africa. Thus, despite the political turmoil in South Africa and the fact that democracy was imminent, it seems as if many *madāris* in the country implemented a minimalist view of Islamic education corroborated by such institutions' overemphasis on rote learning at the expense of critical understanding. Similarly, the apparent reluctance on the part of several religious leaders and *madrassah* teachers to connect *madrassah* education to the challenges posed by apartheid repression and exclusion are indicative of a minimalist view of Islamic education which seemed to have influenced *madāris* during the apartheid period. This brings me to a discussion of a limited case study I conducted during the post-apartheid period (in 2008) to illustrate that Islamic education in *madāris* has shown some tendencies towards connecting with maximalist views on Islamic education, especially regarding the cultivation of an ethical community. I am not suggesting by implication that Islamic education during the apartheid years was practised exclusively along minimalist lines. There is ample evidence to suggest the contrary. For instance, prominent Muslim student organisations such as the Muslim Youth Movement (MYM) and the Muslim Students' Association of South Africa (MSA) advocated a view of Islamic education which connected maximally with the destruction of apartheid, and which influenced some Muslim schools. *Madāris* like Al-Jāmi`a in the Western Cape, for example, were influenced by anti-apartheid religious leaders such as the late Imām Abdullah Haron who died at the hands of the apartheid security police while being imprisoned by the apartheid state. However, by far the majority of *madāris* were guided by minimalist understandings of Islamic education during apartheid primarily because of the conformist views of many Muslim religious leaders and *madrassah* teachers. So, the purpose of my empirical investigation was to ascertain if democratic rule in South Africa and a new education system had impacted the *madāris*. Next I show that this was indeed the case.

Today's world is rife with xenophobia, suspicion, animosity, ethnic hatred, crime and violence, which undeniably exacerbate the 'frailty of human bonds' (Bauman, 2003). Therefore, we urgently need people who can build institutions (including *madāris*) which can contribute to restoring security, building trust and making meaningful interaction with others possible (Bauman, 2001a: 99). In this section I explore the potential of *madāris* in South Africa to produce 'autonomous individuals' who can cultivate an 'ethical community'—one which places a high premium on remedying the 'discomforts of insecurity' (Bauman, 2001a: 145). Individuals cannot on their own remedy the 'discomforts of insecurity' such as xenophobia, ethnic hatred, crime and violence which currently plague many societies. In the first instance, however, security would remain elusive unless individuals can act autonomously, that is, assume responsibility to make choices and build identities in organic relation with others (Bauman, 1999: 137–138). For example, teachers and learners who do not act autonomously would rarely contribute meaningfully to building educative (communicative) relationships if such relationships are seen as 'ready-made', finished and preordained. By implication, autonomous individuals are responsible persons who interact with others in building socially recognisable identities. Following such a notion of autonomy, Muslim teachers and learners act autonomously when they responsibly choose to build their Islamic identity—an identity they recognise by displaying tolerance and respect towards other faiths.

Only autonomous individuals can potentially engender an ethical community. Why? If an ethical community is to be woven together through 'sharing and mutual care' (Bauman, 2001a: 150), it requires individuals who can act responsibly or autonomously. For Bauman (2001a: 71) an ethical community is different from an aesthetic community, because the latter comes to life for the limited duration of an event, interest or problem around which individuals temporarily rally or against which they struggle, but afterwards such a community dissolves again, having reassured its members about the success of tackling individual problems collectively. For example, when Muslims in a particular residential area temporarily unite in protest against the establishment of a 'shebeen' that sells liquor close to a mosque, they constitute an aesthetic community. According to Bauman (2001a: 71), 'whatever their focal point, the common feature of aesthetic communities is the superficial and perfunctory, as well as transient, nature of the bonds between their participants. The bonds are friable and short-lived.' Such a community, unlike an ethical one, does not have a long-term commitment and tends to disappear the moment that the problem has been resolved. An ethical community is 'woven from long-term commitments, from inalienable rights and unshakeable obligations, which thanks to their anticipated (and better still institutionally guaranteed) durability could be treated as known variables when the future is planned and projects designed. And the commitments…would be of the fraternal sharing kind, reaffirming the right of every member to communal insurance (a warrant of certainty, security and safety) against the errors and misadventures which are the risks inseparable from individual life' (Bauman, 2001a: 72). My contention is that the idea of an ethical community is apposite to South Africa as the country and its people endeavour to move away from its apartheid past towards a long-term commitment of ensuring non-racism, non-sexism and the achievement of social justice in all spheres of private and public life. This would involve providing individual benefits such as social security, income support, education and health care (Miller, 2004: 128).

The purpose of my empirical investigation into some of the practices of *madāris* in the post-apartheid period was to ascertain whether the potential exists for individuals to act autonomously, which would invariably position them favourably to contribute to cultivating an ethical community—one which requires that individuals have in mind the long-term commitment of living together and acting collectively. Bauman (2001b: 138–139) offers an account of education aimed at 'preparing [individuals] for life' rather than to 'rationalise the world'. This idea of education is aimed at cultivating autonomous individuals who can live and act together in an ethical community. It means 'cultivating the ability [in individuals] to live daily and at peace with uncertainty and ambivalence, with a variety of standpoints and the absence of unerring and trustworthy authorities;…instilling tolerance of difference and the will to respect the right to be different;…fortifying critical and self-critical faculties and the courage needed to assume responsibility for one's choices and their consequences;…[inculcating in individuals a greater concern with] remaining open-ended than with any specific product, and fearing all premature closure more than it shuns the prospect of staying forever inconclusive'. In my view, Bauman's notion of an ethical community is not incongruent with the idea of an Islamic community—a community Muslims should aspire to achieve if they hope to contribute to a peaceful, globalised world of human co-existence.

In Islam, *ummah* (community) comprises individuals actively engaged with the unending struggle and responsibility for the improvement of the economic, social and political aspects of life (Alibasic, 1999: 234). In this sense *ummah* is concerned with a long-term and inconclusive commitment to the improvement of human conditions. Such a community's concern is to maintain 'the freedom and duty of criticism and monitoring of government', to 'accept criticism in good spirit', to facilitate 'peaceful change', and to remain united through consensus and disagreement (Alibasic, 1999: 237, 240, 242, 292)—a clear indication of such a community's obligation to be critical, to develop self-critical attitudes, and to live peacefully. Moreover, community or *ummah* is also concerned with a plurality of human ideas and with not denying the rights of others (Alibasic, 1999: 249, 271)—thus indicating its tolerance of difference. Such an idea of community is commensurate with the notion of an ethical community. My empirical investigation into the practices of some *madāris* was aimed at discovering whether the possibility exists for Islamic education to cultivate such a community—if possible, and I presume it is, the Islamic education cannot be denied its maximalist stances in some of the current *madāris* in post-apartheid South Africa, specifically in the Western Cape.

Through semi-structured interviews in selected *madāris* in the Western Cape I asked questions related to the way that Muslim teachers' teaching connects with cultivating in learners the ability to live at peace with uncertainty and ambivalence, to exercise tolerance of difference, to fortify critical and self-critical attitudes, to assume responsibility for their choices and the consequences and to remain open-ended and inconclusive. It is to a discussion of these issues that I now turn.

I have argued that during the apartheid years Islamic education in South African *madāris* seem to have been dominated heavily by minimalist views on Islamic education which gave rise to a lack of teacher autonomy, an overemphasis on rote learning at the expense of critical thinking, and a resistance to the idea of an intersubjective community, all of which made critical engagement with the other very unlikely (Waghid, 1994: 21–24). After the demise of apartheid education in public schools in 1995, education policy shifted towards the implementation of a new outcomes-based education (OBE) system which required that learners become actively engaged in the education process, thus resulting in an emphasis on critical thinking and collaborative engagement in the teaching and learning processes. This transformation in the public schooling system was enthusiastically received at the, because the *madāris* always adapted their activities to what happened in the public schools. Also, since some Muslim teachers in the public schools had links with the *madāris* (either as teachers in the *madāris* or as members of the *madrassah* boards), the new demands of outcomes-based education made their way into the *madāris*. For this reason, I wanted to ascertain how much the *madāris* had changed since the days of apartheid education and whether Islamic education in *madāris* has the potential to contribute to enhancing South Africa's newly found democracy. This meant that I had to ask questions related to the implementation of dialogical ways of teaching and learning (or a lack thereof) in the *madāris* after 1994. Through a very limited pilot study involving forty *madrassah* teachers I conducted research on the possibility of *madāris* contributing towards the cultivation of an ethical community, especially also after the events of 9/11 that focused more attention on the *madāris* as the possible seedbeds of terrorism.

Normatively speaking, Islamic education involves three main aspects: getting to know Allāh through rationality; choosing to follow the principles of Islam on the basis of individual and rational choice; and acting rationally in such a way as to provide reasons for why one adheres to the teachings of the Qurān and Sunnah (Bagheri & Khosravi, 2006). These constitutive features of Islamic education, namely rational belief, individual choice and justifiable action, influence the ways teaching and learning manifested (as I have shown) in the early *madāris*. Undeniably, Islamic education has been used throughout the Muslim world to indoctrinate learners (Bagheri & Khosravi, 2006: 100). Yet, on analysing the transcripts of interviews conducted with forty *madrassah* teachers in the Strand-Macassar-Stellenbosch-Wellington and Grassy Park-Lotus River-Ottery areas in the Western Cape province of South Africa,[10] I have found that their practices do not always engender doctrinaire education. For the purposes of this book, I have analysed specifically those aspects of non-doctrinaire Islamic education that show some promise of cultivating the idea of an ethical community—thus paving some way towards a maximalist understanding of Islamic education.

Living at peace with uncertainty and ambivalence

According to several teachers, Islamic education in the *madāris* aims to inculcate in learners respect for life, others' property and the rule of law. On this basis it can be claimed that Muslim learners are taught to live peacefully (the constitutive meaning of Islam) and in peaceful co-existence with others in their societies. This view was corroborated by one teacher who claimed that his lessons 'involve a discussion of local and global issues which affect the lives of people in the community, in particular what it means to have respect for the dignity of human life'. This response was given in relation to a question dealing with *jihād* and terrorism. I got the impression that this teacher wanted to get the message across that *jihād* is a struggle against oppression and exploitation rather than a fight through the lauching of terrorist attacks, for instance, against an external enemy like the United States. Another teacher's claim that 'the West's blame on Muslims for terrorism is unfair' is an indication that unjustifiable aggression does not fit well into the vocabulary of *madrassah* teachers, who through their teaching advocate respect for human life, property and the rule of law. So, the argument that *madāris* are the seedbeds of terrorism is unjustified and seemingly not applicable to post-apartheid South African *madāris*.

To come back to the point about respect for life, others' property and the rule of law: one can claim that learners are taught to resolve challenging issues through argumentation and debate. In other words, if a person disagrees with another or finds somebody else's views or criticisms of Islam unacceptable (for example, the Danish cartoonist blasphemy of Prophet Muhammad (SAW)), this does not mean that violence and aggressive behaviour should ensue. When a Muslim teacher was asked how she dealt with this issue in the *madrassah*, she replied that 'her pupils are to be made aware that Islam has many critics and that we should find a non-aggressive way to persuade others of our faith'. This claim clearly supports the view that *madrassah* teachers encourage learners to resolve challenging issues through argumentation and debate rather than by contravening the rule of law or by taking the law into their own hands. This teacher made it clear that 'the *madrassah* children had a peaceful demonstration in the main road against the unfair attack on the Prophet Muhammad (SAW)'. In essence, it does seem as if *madāris* teach learners what it means to live peacefully in an uncertain and ambivalent society.

Exercising tolerance of difference

In some *madāris* learners are taught to recognise and respect the diversity of opinions that exist within Islam, in particular the differences between the majority Sunnism and minority Shi'ism, but also that Muslims, as aptly put by one teacher, 'do not have an exclusive right to salvation...other people (non-Muslims) can also go to Paradise'. Although the Sunni-Shi`i disagreement is a major point of dispute for some Muslim teachers, this does not give Muslims the right to violate the religious freedoms of others, as stated by one teacher. Another teacher made the point that 'Muslims are a minority group in South Africa[11] and cannot enjoy more privileges that others....They also need to be tolerant of different faiths.' This clearly bears out the claim that Muslim learners are taught to exercise tolerance of difference. According to one particular *madrassah* teacher, 'Shi`ism should not be looked upon favourably and the majority Sunnis should strive to challenge it.' However, even this teacher indicated that instead of becoming intolerant towards Shi`ism, one should find arguments to undermine it. Although another teacher felt that the secular government is doing everything against what the Islamic faith demands, 'Muslims should continue to engage them (government) in debate about the abortion and gay marriages acts'. This teacher made it clear that as 'a Muslim minority we cannot expect to be privileged by the state because some non-Muslims do not see anything wrong with consuming alcohol....It is our (Muslims') duty to inform them of the ills of drinking.' In essence, although some *madrassah* teachers are vehemently opposed to state laws which seem to be in conflict with a maximalist view of Islamic education, learners are encouraged to engage the other and to exhibit tolerance rather that to violate the freedoms of others.

Strengthening critical and self-critical attitudes

Islamic education in the *madāris* socialises learners mostly with the basic tenets of Islam, that is, principles of faith such as belief in a monotheistic God, angels, revealed scriptures, prophets, eschatology and distinguishing between good and evil, religious practices including prayer, fasting, giving of alms to the poor, pilgrimage to the Sacred Mosque in Makkah, Qurānic statements and sayings of the Prophet Muhammad (SAW) in relation to living a pious life, and the recitation and memorisation of the entire Qurān or selected chapters from it. Some teachers also encourage learners to learn Islam to complement the knowledge they acquire in the public schools.[12] According to one teacher: 'When I teach I always encourage learners that whatever they learn at school is not separate from their *din* [religion]...to understand the Qurān you need to do subjects like the ones the children do at [public] school.'

In addition to being socialised into an inherited body of Islamic knowledge, learners are also encouraged to be critical. One teacher stressed the importance of creating opportunities for learners to interact with one another and attend to challenging questions: 'They [learners] come with all sorts of questions…mainly challenging issues of their daily lives…the teachers then have to stop with whatever they are busy with to accommodate these questions.' If learners are encouraged to engage with challenging questions, then it would be reasonable to assume that teaching is meant to 'stir up' learners—what Rorty (1999: 127–128) refers to as 'inciting doubt and stimulating imagination'. In an attempt to fortify learners' critical dispositions, one teacher encourages debate, which to some extent also fosters in him a self-critical attitude: 'I actually encourage the older children to come with their questions…I can and do learn from my students, because when they have a question that I cannot answer then I will have to go look up the answers.' This might sound as if the answers are ready-made. However, it could also mean that the Muslim teacher reflects on some of the questions and then attempts to come up with justifiable responses which learners might find palatable and even take into critical scrutiny themselves. This is corroborated by the teacher's claim that he learns from his students—one can possibly learn from others if one takes into consideration their justifications. Another teacher claims that relying only on the lecturing method is unchallenging 'when learners sit and receive knowledge you teach'. This suggests that the teacher is intent on mutually engaging learners, whereby they can connect with and respond to one another. Consequently Halstead's (2004: 517) view that Islamic education does not promote 'independence of thought and personal autonomy' is untenable, because such a claim assumes that learners are not required to think and judge on what is taught in *madāris*. In essence, one can claim that *madāris* do create opportunities for learners to enhance their critical dispositions, although such practices might at times be minimised by a skewed emphasis on the socialisation process which often lends itself to learning by rote. This means that Halstead's claim that Islamic education is mostly faith-oriented, authoritarian and includes indoctrination is also indefensible (Halstead, 2004: 519). Of course, there are moments in *madrassah* teaching which lend themselves to indoctrination. Some *madrassah* teachers acknowledged that 'there is very little time for dialogue and learners have to be taught without questioning'. However, there are other *madrassah* teachers who have extended their curricula beyond matters of faith and doctrinaire thinking towards dealing with issues such as the eradication of poverty, and even the acquisition of entrepreneurial skills required for small business enterprises. The point is, Islamic education in *madāris* is not exclusively about indoctrination but attempts are made to develop the critical capacities of learners.

Assuming responsibility for individual choice

Madrassah teachers were quite emphatic about Muslims' responsibility to 'choose between right and wrong'. It is a basic principle of Islam that Allāh Almighty has given people the faculty of reasoning to decide between appropriate and inappropriate action. One of the teachers stated that 'Muslims should choose between good and evil…It is their (individual) choice although Allāh Almighty expects of us to do good.' By implication, learners are taught to assume responsibility for their own choices and actions. One teacher also referred to the abuse of drugs by some Muslims and remarked that 'parents cannot always be held responsible for the acts of their children…they (children) have to assume responsibility for the choices they make in life'. This clearly indicates that teaching in the *madāris* emphasises the importance of exercising responsibility for individual choice.

Remaining open-ended and inconclusive

All the *madrassah* teachers considered the Qurān and Sunnah (life experiences of the Prophet Muhammad (SAW)) as necessary to live a good life. Although many felt that the Qurān and Sunnah ought to be lived out uncritically, some thought that the primary sources have to be interpreted contextually, that is, in relation to the circumstances that prevail. One teacher stated that 'the primary sources of Islamic education should be interpreted flexibly in relation to the socio-historical circumstances which affect the lives of Muslims'. This, for some teachers, implies that Islamic education is open-ended and inconclusive, that is, as new situations unfold so the sources of Islam have to be interpreted accordingly. So, the fact that all *madrassah* teachers indicated the axiomatic position of the Qurān and Sunnah does not necessarily mean that its interpretations should be monolithic. Of course, many teachers indicated that Islamic education ought to rely on the interpretive works of exegetical scholars. In other words, it is important for these teachers who rely on the exegeses of prominent Islamic scholars for an understanding of Islamic education, but it does not necessarily mean that their interpretations should be accepted as 'ready-made' and not subjected to further elucidation. One teacher remarked 'that during the time of the great scholars HIV and AIDS was not present. So, the views of such scholars on medical advances are limited and should be subjected to further interpretation.' In this way, interpretations of the primary sources of Islamic education seem to be inconclusive. This makes sense, considering that Muslims believe Islam to be a religion for all times and, as new information becomes available in changing times, so should imaginative (re)interpretations be harnessed.

Thus far I have shown that Islamic education in selected South African *madāris* is not just intent on socialising learners with predetermined teachings of the Qurān and Sunnah. Learners are also taught what it means to live at peace with uncertainty and ambivalence, to exercise tolerance of difference, to fortify critical and self-critical attitudes, to assume responsibility for their choices and its consequences and to remain open-ended and inconclusive—all aspects of Islamic education which link strongly with the cultivation of an ethical community. Certainly from this pilot study it seems very unlikely that *madāris* in South Africa could be accused of breeding terrorists; this is evident from the fact that Islamic education seems to be aimed mostly at producing autonomous individuals who can contribute to addressing the social, economic and political challenges faced by the country and its people.

As has been mentioned earlier, an ethical community has in mind the achievement of long-term commitments based on fraternal sharing and communal engagement against human insecurity and the uncertainty of our times. It is with the cultivation of an ethical Islamic community that *madāris* have the potential to contribute to what Bauman (2001a: 145) calls seeking 'a remedy for the discomforts of insecurity in a care for safety, that is for the integrity of your body with all its extensions and frontline trenches— your home, your possessions, your neighbourhood'. At the time of writing this book, some signs in this regard already appeared as *madāris* in township communities organised collective protest marches with non-Muslims to express their resistance to drug abuse. One teacher remarked: 'We need to educate through collective action our outrage against the use of drugs which not only threatens our community's safety in the long run, but also makes our destiny more and more uncertain.' My contention is that the *madrassah* has a prominent role to play in building relations of trust with others, restoring security in our communities and engendering morally worthwhile human interaction. Selected South African *madāris* in the post-aprtheid period are beginning to show some promise in cultivating what Bauman (2001a: 150) refers to as 'a community of concern and responsibility'.

Finally, an ethical community can contribute to restoring security, building trust, and encouraging meaningful interaction amongst people, because such a community considers dialogue between cultures as necessary since it would enable them to 'open up to each other and engage in a conversation which may enrich them all and enhance the humanity of their togetherness' (Bauman, 2001a: 142). Opening up to one another would invariably break down the walls and fences which often separate and isolate different people. Opening up means that people would come to recognise others, and respect and tolerate diverse people. It is this recognition of the other, respect for and tolerance of diversity that can go some way in building mutual trust and deliberative engagement—those qualities necessary to restore security in our 'polycultural' environment. I contend that *madāris* (in a maximalist way) are beginning to contribute to harnessing a defence of such a community, although much more work needs to be done towards building the communitarian dream—that is, cultivating an ethical community.

NOTES

[1] Makdisi (1981: 19) also distinguishes between *maktab* and *kuttāb*. The *kuttāb* accommodated learners after they reached the age of ten—that is, after having attended the *maktab*.

[2] The *salawāt* has also later been extended to praises rendered for Muslim pioneers, who, through their painstaking efforts, preserved Islam at the Cape.

[3] A Sufi order associated with Muʻʻn al-Din Muhammad Chisti (d. 1236) of India

[4] A Sufi order founded by Muhammad ibn Ali (1178–1255) of the Ba Alawi tribe in Southern Arabia

[5] This means teacher or leader in early Islam at the Cape.

6   Used to refer to either a teacher or a religious leader who has studied in an Arab country

7   Muslims are expected to render prayers five times a day. These prayers are the early morning prayer (*fajr*), the mid-afternoon prayer (*thur*), the late afternoon prayer (`*asr*), the sunset prayer (*maghrib*) and the evening prayer (`*isha*).

8   The Tabligh movement is a missionary movement aimed at propagating Islam in a passive way. This movement is supported by the Deoband trend, for the reason that its teachers were scholars of the Deobandis.

9   This does not mean that rote learning and memorisation are unique to Shafi`i *madāris* only, and that Hanafi-orientated *madāris* are exonerated where rote learning and memorisation are concerned. This is not the case. Rote learning and memorisation are raised as a problem under the discussion of Shafi`i *madāris* because the first *madāris* at the Cape used Shafi`i principles, where teaching and learning was organised in terms of rote and memorisation. Also, rote learning and memorisation *per se* are not uneducative, but if these are the only means of learning, then it leaves no room for creative and independent thinking—an essential concept in education.

10 These *madrassahs* are responsible for teaching 8 to 18-year-old learners. These learners attend public school during the day from 08:00 until 15:00 and attend *madrassah* after 15:00 until 17:00 or 17:30.

11 Almost 2 million Muslims out of a population of approximately 42 million people

12 *Madrassah* classes are offered mostly in the late afternoon (between 15:00 and 17:30) after learners have attended the public school.

CHAPTER 4

Towards maximalist notions of Islamic education

In the previous chapter I discussed the cultivation of an ethical community as a necessary outcome of a maximalist understanding of Islamic education. In this chapter I shall make an argument for peace (*salām*), compassion (*rahmah*) and happiness (*sa'ādah*) as outcomes of Islamic education which would invariably enhance its maximalist position with reference to some of plausible views in the contemporary era.

Islamic education and peace (*salām*) discourses

Most proponents of and adherents to Islamic education, whether their approach is minimalist or maximalist, agree that the primary goal of Islamic education is to achieve universal peace 'deeply anchored in core Islamic values of tolerance for diversity, justice, compassion, and human dignity' (Crow, 2000: 58). Views that Islamic education adheres to doctrinaire understandings such as for Muslims to maintain perennial hostile relations with non-Muslims, and that *sharī'ah* (Islamic legal theory and practice) opposes the pursuit of peaceful human coexistence, are indefensible and not necessarily Islamically inspired. Islamic education does 'not preclude the existence of the other, non-Muslim, nations or international cooperation for the pursuit of security, peace, human rights, development, and the well-being of humanity as a whole' (Baderin, 2000: 59). The promotion of peaceful human coexistence as a primary objective of Islamic education is grounded in a plethora of Qurānic verses which advocate peace on the basis of sincerity, equity, righteousness and piety: 'The (faithful) slaves of the Beneficent are they who walk upon the earth modestly, and when the foolish ones address them answer: Peace' (*al-Furqān*: 63); 'And if two parties or groups among the believers fall to fighting, then make peace between them both, But if one of them outrages against the other, then fight you (all) against the one that which outrages till it complies with the Command of Allāh; then if it complies, then make reconciliation between them justly, and be equitable. Verily! Allāh loves those who are equitable' (al-Hujurāt: 9); and 'Wherewith Allāh guides all those who seek His Good Pleasure to ways of peace, and He brings them out of darkness by His Will unto light and guides them to a Straight Way (Islamic Monotheism)' (al-Māidah: 16). In fact, the first Islamic state in Madinah was established in an era of, firstly, internal peaceful coexistence between Muslims, Jews and local tribesmen and, secondly, external peaceful coexistence with other nations, unlike the pre-Islamic warmongering traditions of the Arabs (Baderin, 2000: 61). Islamic education's inclination towards peace also finds support in the following verses: 'But if they incline to peace, you also incline to it, and (put your) trust in Allā. Verily, He is the All-Hearer, the All-Knower' (al-Anfāl: 61); and 'And if a woman fears cruelty or desertion on her husband's part, there is no sin on them both if they make terms of peace between themselves; and making peace is better. And human inner-selves are swayed by greed. But if you do good and keep away from evil, verily, Allā is Ever Well-acquainted with what you do' (al-Nisā: 128). Siddiqui aptly (2001: 71) claims that 'Islam is derived from the Arabic word salām, meaning peace. Islam has thus been translated as meaning the attainment of peace through submission to Allāh. The goal of the Islamic way of life is to achieve peace at all levels—spiritual, social, political and economic. The Islamic system and laws thus seek to promote, protect, and sustain peace.'

I shall now show how Islamic education's rationale of cultivating peaceful human relations can be engendered along the lines of caring for others, embarking upon tolerant action, and respecting human rights. Firstly, the Qurān contains verses such as the following, which articulate the multiple ways in which Allāh communicates with human beings: 'It is not given to any human being that Allah should speak to him unless (it be) by Revelation, or from behind a veil, or (that) He sends a Messenger to reveal what He wills by His Leave. Verily, He is Most High, Most Wise' (al-Shūrā: 51). My interest in divine-human interaction is not so much in the manner in which Allāh communicates with human beings, whether through inspiration, from behind a veil, or by sending a messenger, but rather the reason for such communication. Considering the inspirational mode of divine-human interaction, such as Allāh's interaction with the mother of Moses, with Abraham and with David, I want to argue that these modes of inspirational communication are inextricably connected with the notion of caring, that is, evoking the potentialities of the 'recipients' of the divine message. As the Qurān states: 'And We inspired the mother of Mūsa (Moses), (telling): Suckle him [Mūsa (Moses)], but when you fear for him, then cast him into the river and fear not, nor grieve. Verily! We shall bring him back to you, and shall make him one of (Our) Messengers' (al-Qasas: 7). Similarly, in communication with Abraham, Allāh states: 'And, when he (his son) was old enough to walk with him, he said: O my son! I have seen in a dream that I am slaughtering you (offer you in sacrifice to Allah), so look what you think! He said: O my father! Do that which you are commanded, Insha` Allāh (if Allāh wills), you shall find me of As-Sābirūn (the patient) (al-Sāfāt: 102). In the case of Moses, his mother was told to 'suckle' him and thereafter to cast him into the river, whereas, in the case of Abraham, he was asked to work with his son, then before offering him in sacrifice, to solicit his opinion. In both instances, parents were instructed to nurture (tarbiyyah) their children, and then to encourage them to act autonomously after having consulted with them or initiated procedures for engagement.

In relation to Islamic education, the point about caring as a way to cultivate peaceful human relations is that it is not enough for a Muslim teacher to be affectionate towards or to be attached to others, which caring promotes. One has to be affectionate towards or attached to a student in order to care. But this does not mean that one merely has to please a student even if one's actions are not in his or her best interest. A student might want to go canoeing on a tranquil lake. Later on she might want to take part in a canoe race down a swollen river without having been educated to manoeuvre the canoe or to cope with winds and other inclement weather conditions. It would please the student if you were to allow her to paddle a canoe on a raging river, but it might not be in the best interest of her safety. If one is really to acquire the virtue of caring for others and not just being affectionate towards them, one needs to cultivate in others the capacity to reach their own justifiable conclusions to which they are to be held accountable by and to others for those conclusions MacIntyre (1999: 83) speaks of the ability to evaluate, modify or reject one's own practical judgements. To use a metaphor: the student is 'taught' the procedures regarding entering and leaving, paddling, steering and portaging (carrying) a canoe. She is also informed about the seasonal conditions that need to be taken into account when canoeing, she is 'taught' to paddle skilfully and she is coached about making difficult decisions in inclement weather. When she has gone through this process, she has been initiated into a practice of evaluating, modifying and rejecting her judgements concerning handling a canoe. The student is cared for if she received good education about canoeing and if she was properly guided to acquire ways of discovering her own version of the sport. In turn the student will act prudently.

To continue the metaphor: the teachers (parents or trainers) of the student who received a good education in canoeing did not just impose on her their own understanding of canoeing, but allowed her the freedom of choice to reflect on and to modify and sustain the practice of handling a canoe (similar to the freedom Abraham's son was given). The student developed the capacity to make practical judgements when she encounters unforeseen situations while canoeing; she would rationally make decisions that would not necessarily endanger her life and the lives of other competitors; and after every major canoeing event she would re-educate herself so as to become more competitive in canoe racing. Caring then, does not merely involve cultivating in ourselves 'degrees of affection' towards others but we also demonstrate caring through encouraging others to develop their capacities of evaluation and modification, that is, what others consider to be sufficiently good reasons for acting. This will enable them to imagine alternative possibilities and consequently to rationally re-educate themselves to become practical reasoners (MacIntyre, 1999: 83).

By implication, Muslim teachers care for learners when they (teachers) encourage learners to develop capacities of evaluation and modification, that is, when learners are taught to become reflective and independent members of their societies and are imbued with virtues that allow them to act imaginatively as individuals and members of groups. In this regard MacIntyre and Dunn (2002: 3) make the point that 'contemporary teachers have the task of educating their students, so that those students will bring to the activities of their adult life questioning attitudes that will put them at odds with the moral temper of the age and with its dominant institutions'. (In this way, learners' cognitive skills would not only be enhanced, but also nurtured in a maximalist way. What follows from the aforementioned discussion about caring is that Islamic education has the best chance of realising its goal of cultivating peaceful human relations if learners are taught to care, that is, if they are taught to maximise their potentialities in the interest of a just cause. I cannot imagine Islamic education without the notion of caring (whereby the potentialities of learners are invoked) being cultivated, or without being attentive to societal problems of drug and alcohol abuse, racial and ethnic prejudice, the sexual debasement of women and children, the depletion of natural resources, and universal ecological concerns. For Muslim teachers and learners to adopt an ethic of care would potentially open up peace discourses of a non-violent nature. People who are taught to care in the sense developed here would realise that Islamic education does not merely involve an understanding that piety and religion will effect real change in society, but also that human beings should not be detached from the burning issues of democracy, freedom of expression, women's rights, and modernity that confront them. Then, proponents of peace or carers would begin to think intelligently and to act wisely.

Secondly, it cannot be denied that the world today is marked by undisputed diversity, whether it be religious, political, cultural or moral. Yet, if we want to ensure peace and human co-existence as human beings we somehow have to put up with one another's differences. Of course, some of us might be intent on causing bitter conflict because we might disapprove of somebody else's religious, ethnic, sexual, cultural or moral orientation. Consequently we might attempt to suppress others' differences, thus disturbing peaceful co-existence and at times even making it impossible to for others to exist (Sahin, 2007: 5). Examples of this kind of behaviour are ethnic and religious intolerance in northern Africa, resulting in fierce conflict, racism in the Democratic Republic of the Congo, resulting in rape and the mass murder of Tutsi women and children by Hutu militia, and recent xenophobic clashes in South Africa, ending in point blank shootings and assassinations of Muslim Somali shopkeepers. These are all moments of profound intolerance which undermine the peaceful co-existence of diverse peoples. To my mind, Islamic education in a maximalist way cultivates in people the capacity for tolerant behaviour which is not contrary to the Qurānic injunction, 'Unto you your religion, and unto me my religion' (al-Kāfirūn: 6). Tolerance towards others, whether their ways of living are starkly different to one's own, is not out of step with the primary sources of Islamic education and hence, a maximalist view of Islamic education.

For me, putting up with somebody else's differences does not mean that one necessarily approves or disapproves of the practices of that person. If one happens to approve of the practices of someone else, then one agrees with the practices of someone else, for instance, approving of one's neighbour's sexual preferences is tantamount to agreeing with such a practice. Similarly, disapproving of someone else's beliefs or orientations implies some expression of disagreeing with someone. Tolerance is not about approving or disapproving of someone else's preferences; neither is it about accepting or rejecting others' moral commitments or diverse understandings of the good life. Rather, tolerance involves creating conditions whereby others can live their competing differences without being coercively interfered with, hindered or prohibited from exercising their life choices. In this regard, I concur with Sahin (2007: 5) who posits that tolerance involves creating 'a private sphere for individuals and groups in which they can express their differences, and a window of opportunity through which the differences may come to be respected by all parties in the long run'. Allowing someone else to live their differences is different from approving or even disapproving of such differences. And, engaging with the differences of others whereby the possibility remains open for respect of such differences does not necessarily mean that one also approves or disapproves of their differences. I can engage with someone else's religious beliefs which might be different to mine, but this does not mean that I approve or disapprove of their beliefs. I tolerate differences because I want to prevent any ensuing destructive conflict and persecution which might threaten peaceful co-existence. In fact, tolerance leaves a self-determined space for individuals to determine their own understanding of the good life, their moral autonomy (Sahin, 2007: 15). Such a view of tolerance accords with the spirit of diversity suggested by Prophet Muhammad's (SAW) statement that 'difference of opinion within my community is a sign of Allāh's mercy' (Sahin, 2007: 15). Hence, tolerance through Islamic education is aimed at securing the right of dissent and protecting people from interference in their affairs. In other words, tolerance is a condition of human behaviour whereby Sikh men can wear their headgear freely, Jewish men a yarmulka, and Muslim women a *hijāb* in public spaces. The point about tolerance is that it can ensure peaceful human co-existence which is far more important to humanity's cultivation than being concerned about coercing others into some homogeneous collectivity.

However, to be tolerant does not necessarily imply apathy. Neither does tolerance mean that one has to be satisfied with injustices perpetrated against humanity. Tolerance ceases when injustices towards others are committed. I cannot imagine the Qurān being burnt and people (Muslim and non-Muslims) sitting back without opposing such a form of religious intolerance, neither can I imagine synagogues and churches being destroyed, or the *minārats* of mosques being removed if these are all religious symbols which determine people's ways of being. Here the *Hadīth* of the Prophet Muhammad (SAW), 'Whoever observes an injustice should change it with his (her) hand, and if he or she is unable to do so then change should be brought through articulation of speech (tongue), and if he or she fails, then through silence (heart)', is quite apposite. I am very reluctant to assume that 'hand' signifies the use of force. Instead, I am inclined to suggest that 'hand' signifies an invitation to engage with others through speech and peaceful resistance. In a way, engaging others with some kind of belligerent ('handful') speech in order to substantiate one's argument against offensive behaviour is not necessarily inappropriate. Yet, in all situations of belligerent rebuttal and deliberative engagement about the truths of one's religious beliefs, violence should never be an option.

I agree with Arendt, who claims that 'the practice of violence, like all action, changes the world, but the most probable change is to a more violent world' (1969: 80). In this sense, although the temporary use of violence has been justified, it does not make violence legitimate. Why not? In the first place, the use of violence against people can cause innocent bystanders to lose their lives. This means that the perpetrators of violence disrespect the lives of others who might not necessarily have been responsible for an undesirable situation. I cannot imagine that all people in the New York Twin Towers, the London tubes, the Oklahoma World Trade Centre, and Baghdad were responsible for an undesirable situation which some people found offensive and worthy of violent self-destructive actions, that is, 'suicide bombings'. And, seeing that those who were subjected to violence suffered such human indignity, torture and aggression were innocent, the use of violence cannot be considered to be legitimate. In support of this view, Arendt (1969: 52) posits that:

> Violence can be justifiable, but it never can be legitimate. Its justification loses in plausibility the farther its intended end recedes into the future. No one questions the use of violence in self-defence, because the danger is not only clear but present, and the end justifying the means is immediate.

It seems important to bear in mind that violence as an act of aggression against people might be justifiable, but its legitimacy can be questioned on the basis that the very act of violence aims to annihilate, hurt or cause some sort of discomfort to people whom one might find unwilling to engage in dialogical action. In other words, the act of causing physical and emotional harm to anyone cannot be legitimate because violence is meant to let the other experience suffering and pain. I say this because legitimate action has some connection with what others agree should happen to them. In this way, by not agreeing to be violently assaulted, their human dignity somehow remains intact. This kind of violence is different from violence used in self-defence, as noted by Arendt. If I defend myself against those who perpetrate violence against me, then my violent retaliation or defence becomes legitimate only if I am willing to cease with my defence once the perpetrator of violence against me decides to end the violence. In other words, legitimacy only has currency if I defend myself against violent acts and restrain my actions once others have ceased their violence. Consequently, the argument that violence can never be legitimate is a conditional one: self-defence against acts of violence is justifiable and legitimate when I restrain myself after the initial perpetrator of violence has ceased all acts of violence against me. For instance, when the armed wing of the African National Conference (Umkhonto we Sizwe) defended itself against the political killings of the apartheid state, their violent self-defence was only justifiable and hence legitimate until the apartheid government ceased the perpetration of violence against members of the liberation movement.

It follows from this that if Islamic institutions encourage people *solely* to use self-destructive ways of ending the lives of others to instil fear in the hearts and minds of those left behind then such use of violence becomes illegitimate. This is so because fear, control and compliance are the intended ends of such violent acts that are undesirable for any form of human interaction and interdependence and to which very few people would agree. If they do so for the sake of self-defence against a violent perpetrator then their responses become conditionally legitimate. Therefore Arendt (1969: 51) is correct when she states that 'violence is by nature instrumental; like all means, it always stands in need of guidance and justification through the end it pursues'. In this way the use of violence in itself remains illegitimate, but its use as self-defence makes it conditionally legitimate on the grounds that self-defence will end once perpetrated acts of violence against one have ceased. For instance, Umkhonto we Sizwe ended its violent campaign once the apartheid state agreed to enter into dialogue with its 'enemy'.

Thirdly, jurists have categorised rights in Islamic theology as follows: rights of Allāh (*huqūq al-Allāh*) or divine commands such as the right to perform prayer, fasting and hajj (pilgrimage); rights shared by Allāh and His servants (*huqūq al-Allāh wal `ibād*), demanded by Allāh and intended to serve the public, such as *hudūd* (penal law), *zakāt* (charity) and *jihād* (striving in Allāh's cause); and rights of Allāh's servants (*huqūq al-`ibād*), the rights intended to protect individual interests, such as fulfilling promises, paying back debts and honouring contracts (Sāfi, 2001: 2). Now respect for human rights in Islam is intertwined in the aforementioned categories of divine, political and legal rights. At the core of such an understanding of rights is, firstly, that one exercises one's individual right when one has the liberty to autonomously make one's choices and to be held accountable for one's actions—as stated in the Qurān: '…that no bearer of burdens can bear the burden of another' (*al-Najm:* 38); and secondly, that one ought to respect the rights of others who might hold different views or adhere to different moral choices than oneself—as confirmed in the Qurān: 'Certainly your efforts and deeds are diverse (different in aims and purposes)' (*al-Layl*: 4); and thirdly, that others should reciprocate and respect one's choices—as stated in the Qurān: 'If it had been the Lord's Will they would all have believed all who are on earth! Wilt thou then compel mankind against their will to believe?' (*Yūnūs*: 99). To exercise one's right thus involves four aspects: (1) the fact of agency, that is, a capacity to make a choice; (2) one's ability to carry out choices without the interference of others; (3) one's possession of the means for carrying out one's choices; and (4) self-development, which amounts to the autonomous formation of one's character and being able to carry out long-term projects (Christiano, 1990: 153). Now surely an individual, for instance, exercising her right to freedom of expression, cannot be allowed to engage in verbal or physical vandalism, such as waging insults against church, synagogue or mosque congregants or even vandalising religious buildings—actions which not only subvert the rights of others to freedom of religious practice or security of person, but also disrupt the communal values of social co-existence and recognition of diverse religious persuasions. In other words, the preservation of communal values such as respect for diversity, recognition of the rights of others and tolerance towards different faiths, enjoins the individual to exercise her rights within limits, whereas transgressing such values will result in undermining the freedoms of others. The point I am making is that the expression of private (atomistic) individual freedoms cannot be allowed unless there is overwhelming evidence that such expressions cannot be detrimental to other individuals belonging to a community. This is because although freedoms belong primarily to individuals, their exercise will directly or indirectly affect other members of a community. Put differently: individuals' freedoms are exercised in the context of relationships with others, not as isolated, absolute individualistic expressions.

From the aforementioned, it can be inferred that a person is said to have a right, to be a rights holder, 'when he (she) has a claim, the recognition of which is called for—not (necessary) by legal rules—but by moral principles, or principles of an enlightened conscience' (Feinberg, 1972: 67). There are two distinct notions of rights at play here: on the one hand, an atomistic view of rights, whereby individuals conceive of themselves as independent holders of rights which preclude them from the opportunity to be genuinely committed to a sense of community. On the other hand, there is the view that rights ought to be committed to the claim that individuals should always bear their rights resolutely before them, that is, 'for (the) profound expression of community'—a view that differs from the atomistic view. I shall argue that the popular idea of individual rights with its emphasis only on self-attention is atomistic, and that the pursuit of a notion of individual rights (which is necessary), should not be oblivious of the individual's responsibilities to others and vice versa. Now a central feature of atomistic rights is the notion of negative individual rights of which the basis is the right to the unimpeded development of every human being (Freeden, 1990: 492). In other words, such a view of rights seems to uphold the negative liberty of non-interference by others, that is, it regards the intervention of other individuals or groups as the main impediments to human development, and the sole impediments from which individuals deserve and may claim social protection.

Now how is the notion of negative individual rights supposed to operate within the context of Islamic education? For instance, if everyone has the right to a basic Islamic education then it can be deduced that a person who has been endowed with the creative and imaginative talent of inventiveness has the right to develop such a capacity through her own exertions and efforts—and hence through self-attention attain an appropriate intellectual, economic, social and (perhaps) political status. For, after all, the individual has a right to develop her natural abilities and talents. Thus, arguments against the exercising of intellectual activity on the part of a self-assertive, autonomous individual possessed of the capacity for inventiveness seem absurd. However, if the individual in a self-determining way insists on her rights to invent or do harmful and degrading things, such as making a device ('bomb') in order to inflict harm on people, the possibility of slipping down the slope of selfishness when one is totally obsessed with the notion of the individual right to make bad choices becomes quite real. In this way, an atomistic individual might not show sensitivity to the well-being and interests of others. In any case, as Gyekye (1997: 69) correctly argues, 'one's right not to be harmed imposes a responsibility on others not to harm one'.

Other rights, which do not only depend on the private (atomistic) reasons of the individual but also on the exercising of public reasons, include: 'to stand for public office', 'to an environment that is not harmful to their health or well-being', 'adequate housing' and 'social security' (Gyekye, 1997: 69). To stand for public office might be considered to be a self-attentive individual right and aspiration, but to occupy such a position becomes an inherently social responsibility which involves serving the legitimate interests of others. I am reminded of Rawls's observation in his book *A Theory of Justice* that the right of an individual to 'social security' entails the endorsement by the citizenry (public) of what is of value to human life in a democratic society (Rawls, 1971: 178). The point I am making is similar to that explained by Freeden (1990: 492): on the one hand, negative rights 'present individuals as self-determining, as best capable of preserving their own interests, as indeed self-developing...arguing that each individual is the best judge of his or her development, or life-plan'. Such a view of individual rights seems to embed an atomistic view of rights as has been argued for earlier. On the other hand, my contention is that human beings can only function and give expression to their abilities by means of other individuals. On this account of positive rights, the danger of an atomistic view of individual rights seems to be diminished, that is, 'rights cannot be grounded primarily on the protection of free action from the intervention of others, for such intervention may frequently be regarded as beneficial, desirable, indeed, essential, to the expression of human qualities'

(Freeden, 1990: 493). Unlike what an atomistic view of rights assumes, society itself (comprising other individuals) has rights that could be asserted against individuals (Freeden, 1978: 90). This issue of positive rights is succinctly expressed by Hobhouse (1922: 62–63): '[R]ights must include, in addition to the rights of individual members, the right of the community as a whole.' Hobhouse (1922: 161) expressed the view that 'the community, like the individual, performs certain functions which require their due return, apart from which they would be starved'.

The point about exercising individual rights in an atomistic sense is that such rights have to be limited, especially when destructive action (for instance, suicide bombings) is envisaged. Rights cannot just be exercised in a unilateral and foolish way that could potentially have devastating consequences for society and could pose a serious threat to world peace. Consequently, it is worth noting that the Organisation of Islamic Conference (OIC), founded in February 1973 to initially coordinate cooperation among Muslim states in the economic, social, cultural, scientific and other fields, in its 'Declaration on Dialogue among Civilisation' (May 1999) promotes 'the protection of human rights and human responsibility, including the rights of minorities and migrants to maintain their cultural identity and observe their values and traditions; and [to promote]…the rights of and dignity of women, safeguarding the institution of family, and protection of the vulnerable segments of the human population: the children, the youth and the elderly' (Baderin, 2007: 74). The organisation, which includes almost one-third of the membership of the United Nations, also declared its intent to contribute to the programmes of the United Nations in the following critical areas: building a global order based on inclusion, dialogue, mutual understanding and respect instead of outdated doctrines of exclusion, rivalry, power politics and selfish pursuit of narrow interests; non-resort to war and the threat or use of force in international relations, except in self-defence; global commitment to peaceful settlement of disputes in accordance with principles of justice and international law; the imperative of respect for justice and the rule of law in international relations; recognition of the rights of peoples under alien domination or foreign occupation to self-determination; withdrawal of Israel from occupied territories; commitment to a world free of weapons of mass destruction; eradication of global menaces such as terrorism, organised crime and drug trafficking; and the implementation of equity, transparency and democracy (Baderin, 2007: 75). What follows from the aforementioned discussion of rights is that individuals cannot simply do what they want to do. Rights are exercised in accordance with what is good for society in general, more specifically peaceful relations amongst all peoples. And, if Islamic education hopes to contribute to upholding rights in a maximalist way, it should simultaneously be cautious about advocating for unimpeded individual rights that could undermine world peace, which is the primary aim of Islamic discourses. This brings me to a discussion of Islamic education in relation to compassion.

Islamic education and compassion (*rahmah*)

There is not a single chapter in the Qurān that does not contain the concept *rahmah* (compassion). In addition, Allāh Almighty is also referred to throughout the Qurān, *Hadīth* and others sources of Islamic education as 'The Most Compassionate' (*al-Rahmān*): 'Then will he be of those who believe, and enjoin patience, (constancy, and self-restraint), and enjoin deeds of kindness and compassion' (*al-Balad*: 17); 'For Abraham was, without doubt forbearing (of faults), compassionate, and given to look to Allāh' (*Hūd*: 75); and 'Muhammad is the Messenger of Allāh; and those who are with him are strong against Unbelievers, (but) compassionate amongst each other. Thou wilt see them bow and prostrate themselves (in prayer) seeking Grace from Allāh and (His) Good Pleasure. On their faces are their marks, (being) the traces of their prostration. This is their similitude in the Towrah; and their similitude in the Gospel is: like a seed which sends forth its blade, then makes it strong; it then becomes thick and it stands on its own stem (filling) the sowers with wonder and delight. As a result, it fills the Unbelievers with rage at him. Allāh has promised those among them who believe and do righteous deeds Forgiveness and a great Reward' (*al-Fath*: 29). What follows from this is that Islamic education is inextricably connected with the cultivation of compassion.

Nussbaum (2001) raises the question of what positive contribution emotions such as compassion can make in guiding deliberation amongst learners, in this instance, those in *madāris*. Her main argument in defence of compassion is that it ought to be the emotion which should be most frequently cultivated when people embark upon rational deliberation and just action in public as well as private life (Nussbaum, 2001: 299). In her view, rational deliberation ought to be occasioned by the emotion to treat others justly and humanely—with compassion. Certainly in South African *madāris*, where diverse learners (from both indigenous and immigrant communities) are beginning to deliberate about matters of public concern such as crime, victimisation, homelessness, job discrimination, unemployment, domestic violence and abuse of women, poverty and lack of food, political alienation, alcoholism and drug abuse, and absence of good prospects, they have to make certain practical judgements about these variants of their public and personal lives. Invariably judgements to be made will be based on learners' perceptions of others' distress, undeserved misfortune, suffering, injustice, plight, disability and disease. It is in this regard that compassion becomes a necessary condition to deliberate about such matters. Why? Compassion not only prompts in people an awareness of the misfortune or suffering of others, but also 'pushes the boundaries of the self' (Nussbaum, 2001) outward by focusing on others' suffering which might be caused through no fault of their own.

Nussbaum's (2001) understanding of compassion as painful emotional judgement embodies at least two cognitive requirements: firstly, a belief or appraisal that the suffering of others is serious and not trivial and that persons do not deserve the suffering; and secondly, the belief that the possibilities of the person who experiences the emotion are similar to those of the sufferer. I shall now discuss these two requirements of compassion in relation to how *madrassah* learners and teachers ought to deliberate rationally, while also cultivating the concern to be just and humane towards others—to be compassionate.

Firstly, insofar as one can become serious about the suffering of others, one needs to believe that they are not to blame for the kind of (undeserved) injustice they might have suffered, and one should recognise that the person's plight needs to be alleviated. Many learners who are perhaps blameless for their inability to pay school fees because their parents did not have the benefit of economic prosperity require the compassion of others. In such circumstances, deliberation at the *madrassah* should rather take the form of ascertaining what could be done to ensure that learners who do not have the finances to study remain part of the *madrassah* community, rather than finding ways to penalise or at times humiliate them. So compassion requires blamelessness on the part of learners who are unable to pay fees, as well as 'onlookers' who can make judgements about the need to expedite the flourishing of the learners in question. Similarly, a teacher has compassion for learners with an impoverished schooling background not necessarily of their own creation (parents could not have afforded to send children to more affluent and organised *madāris*, or to employ private teachers who come to their homes, as is the case in South Africa). Such a teacher recognises the need to find creative ways of assisting disadvantaged learners to come to grips with difficult concepts in their studies and at the same time acknowledges that the minimalist Islamic education system to which some these learners might have been exposed is no fault of their own. One could argue that all learners should be treated equally and that no learner should receive preferential treatment in terms of additional pedagogical support. But then this would be to ignore the undeserved unequal Islamic education many learners, certainly in South Africa, have been or might still be subjected to.

Secondly, compassion is best cultivated if one acknowledges some sort of community between oneself and the other, understanding what it might mean for one to encounter possibilities and vulnerabilities similar to those of the sufferer: '[One] will learn compassion best if he [she] begins by focusing on their sufferings' (Nussbaum, 2001: 317). Again, 'in order for compassion to be present, the person must consider the suffering of another as a significant part of his or her own scheme of goals and ends. She must take that person's ill as affecting her own flourishing. In effect, she must make herself vulnerable in the person of another' (Nussbaum, 2001: 319). What this recognition of one's own related vulnerability means is that learners who might have a clear understanding of, say, concepts in a *madrassah* classroom and become impatient with their peers for not grasping such concepts, should imagine what it would mean for them to encounter difficulty with concepts. Likewise, a *madrassah* teacher should become more aware of what it means for learners to encounter epistemological difficulty. In the words of Nussbaum (2001: 319), 'the recognition of one's own related vulnerability is, then, an important and frequently an indispensable epistemological requirement for compassion in human beings'.

In essence, compassion brings to the fore the intellectual emotions of people in ethical deliberation. It is simply not sufficient to educate by just focusing on reasoning without also cultivating compassion. Reasoning prompts learners and teachers to question meanings, imagine alternative possibilities, modify practical judgements and foster respect and critical engagement. Yet, it seldom brings into play those emotions of people that are necessary to make it worthwhile to continue the engagement. If one is going to ignore the pedagogical vulnerabilities of the weak, very little will be done in the direction of meaningful and maximalist Islamic education. So we also need compassionate learners and teachers. But compassion in relation to *madāris* without also taking into account the lived experiences of those who suffer in our society would constrain relevant Islamic education that aims to improve the conditions of the marginalised other. Hence I shall focus below on practical strategies, once again drawing on the thoughts of Nussbaum, that teachers in *madāris* can use to engender compassionate, and thus maximalist, Islamic education.

Nussbaum's compelling account of compassionate education articulates practical strategies that *madrassah* could employ to support and cultivate a maximalist form of Islamic education—that is, an Islamic education for compassion. Firstly, compassionate education for Nussbaum (2001: 426) involves cultivating in learners the ability to imagine the experiences of others and to participate in their sufferings—to extend their empathy to more people and types of people. This can already be done at an elementary level (*maktab*) when learners learn their first stories, rhymes and songs, in particular through seeking out works that acquaint the learner with a sense of wonder—a sense of mystery that blends curiosity with surprise. Think of a story that begins with, 'Imagine there are no people…and that Muslims should feed the poor.' In learning the story, the learner learns to imagine what life would be like without other human beings and psychologically develops a concern for people outside herself. Later on, she may also be encouraged to notice the suffering of people with a new keenness which might cause her to be exposed to other stories that display the vulnerabilities of human life—death, illness, rape, war, deceit and tragedy. As far as tragedy is concerned, Nussbaum (2001: 428) argues that tragedies acquaint learners with bad things that may happen in human life long before life itself does so, thus enabling a concern for others who are suffering what she has not suffered. For instance, through myth, storytelling, poetry, drama, music and works of art, teachers could acquaint learners with a wide range of possible calamities and other important aspects of life that make people vulnerable. This approach could encourage learners to become attentive to and concerned about the distress that human beings can experience. Novels about the fate of a tragic and worthy hero, the trauma of young women raped in wartime, the murder of children, the experiences of the mentally disabled, and people who have suffered from the hatred of those in power could be used by *madrassah* teachers as powerful sources of 'compassionate imagining' (Nussbaum, 2001: 430).

Secondly, an Islamic education for compassion should also be a multicultural education. This involves an education (through the teaching of indigenous languages and literature, social sciences, and life orientation curricula in South Africa) which acquaints learners with a rudimentary understanding of the histories and cultures of many different people, that is, major religious and cultural groups, as well as ethnic, racial and social majorities and minorities in terms of sexual orientation. Awareness of cultural difference is necessary in order to engender respect for one another, which is an essential underpinning for compassionate Islamic education. Moreover, Islamic education for compassion needs to begin early. As soon as learners engage in storytelling, they can tell stories about other nations and countries. Certainly in South African *madāris* they could learn that religions other than Islam exist; that people have different ways of thinking, traditions and beliefs.

For instance, one such theme in life orientation (commonly known as *Akhlāq* studies) for *madrassah* learners could involve educating learners about Islamic myths and folktales and the injustices perpetrated against people (Muslims or non-Muslims). By the time they reach university they should be well equipped to deal with demanding courses on human diversity outside the dominant Islamic traditions. The goals of such a theme could be threefold: to develop in learners a sense of informed, compassionate action as they enter the broader society of increasing diversity in terms of race, ethnicity, social class and religious sectarianism; to provide learners with an intellectual awareness of the causes and effects of structured inequalities and prejudicial exclusion in society; and to expand learners' ability to think critically about controversial issues that stem from the gender, race, class, ethnic and religious differences that pervade our society. Nussbaum (2001: 432) supports such a view when she claims: 'Our pupil must learn to appreciate the diversity of circumstances in which human beings struggle for flourishing; this means not just learning some facts about classes, races, nationalities, sexual orientations other than her own, but being drawn into those lives through the imagination, becoming a participant in those struggles'.

In the next section, I shall deal with some of the principles one can use as a *madrassah* teacher in teaching Islamic education for high school students, particularly with regard to how learners can relate their learning to compassionate imagining. The *madrassah* programme ought to be informed by three decisions. The first would be to put reasoning at the heart of the matter, which would awaken critical and independent thinking about values such as deliberative democracy, citizenship, equality and freedom, human rights, and socio-economic and political justice in relation to Islamic education in *madāris*. Learners should engage in a lot of serious discussion of issues related to these themes. The second decision would be to focus the course clearly. Its emphasis should be on lively debate and argumentation among learners rather than on the mere acquisition of facts. There should be earnest deliberation on the above-mentioned themes in group discussions and learners should report to the whole class. Through such an approach active critical engagement could potentially be elicited. Learners should be taught how to challenge one another and to consider alternative interpretations, and they should be stimulated to explore their own thinking on pertinent issues. Then, the Islamic education curriculum should also focus on an area of diversity by selecting different cultural perspectives, say from Muslim and non-Muslim countries. Learners should be encouraged to raise critical issues about race, gender, ethnicity, social class and religious sectarianism. Critical discussion of cultural diversity in different countries should be aimed at enhancing learners' awareness of differences in the beliefs and practices of their own culture, while exploring a foreign culture. The third decision would be to focus on a theme such as 'Poverty, famine and hunger'. Learners should be taught how to think about the relationship of poverty, hunger and famine to distress, undeserved misfortune, suffering, injustice, disability and disease in different parts of the world. More importantly, the Islamic education course should also link critical inquiry to discussions about issues of peace and terrorism. When Islamic education in *madāris* becomes intensely concerned about what Nussbaum (2001: 403) refers to as 'tragic predicaments and their prevention', such institutions embody compassion, since they rely on compassionate learners and teachers to keep alive the essential concern to attend to the well-being of others—a matter of balancing their responsibilities and emotions.

Now that I have explored a maximalist understanding of Islamic education in relation to compassionate imaging, I shall move on to a discussion of Islamic education and its link with happiness.

Islamic education and happiness

Islamic education frames happiness (*sa`ādah*) along two dimensions: the hereafter (*ukhrawiyyah*) and the present world (*dunyawiyya*)—the former being ultimate and everlasting, and the latter being worldly and linked to the former (al-Attas, 1995: 91). Of importance to this analysis of happiness is the notion that the concept is related to knowledge, virtue and good character, good health and security, and those material issues (such as wealth and property) that justly promote the well-being of people (al-Attas, 1995: 91). Deliberate thinking, reflection and freedom of choice are considered as apposite for virtue and good character, and when desire and anger are subordinated to the use of the intellect, justice is said to be realised (al-Attas, 1995: 93). Thus, happiness in Islam is not restricted to temporal life but is also related to the hereafter.

Of importance to my argument is that happiness in this world can be responsive to moral decadence, crisis, misery and conflict (al-Attas, 1995: 95). Happiness in this sense is related to good conduct and virtuous activity (al-Attas, 1995: 108). Also, the Qurān is clear than happiness in the world is related to achieving virtuosity: 'If Allāh touches thee with affliction, none can remove it but He; if He touches thee with happiness, He hath power over all things' (*al-`Anām*: 17); and 'Those who believed (in the Oneness of Allāh—Islamic Monotheism), and work righteousness, Tūba (all kinds of happiness or name of a tree in Paradise) is for them and a beautiful place of (final) return' (*al-Rad*: 29). I want to argue that an important maximalist goal of Islamic education is to achieve happiness in society by linking such happiness to the attainment of democratic justice.

Gutmann (2003) gives a compelling account of democratic justice which can bring about maximalist learning in *madāris*. Gutmann (2003: 26–27) contends that democratic justice involves three interrelated aspects: the capacity to live one's own life as one sees fit, consistent with respecting the equal freedoms of others, that is, 'to treat all individuals as equal agents'; the capacity to contribute to the justice of one's society and one's world; and the capacity of individuals to live a decent life with a fair chance of choosing among their preferred ways of living. Firstly, if one learns to respect the liberties of others and sees them as being as important as one's own, then one recognises that others have similar freedoms to live their lives as they see fit. So, when learners are taught to respect the freedoms of other learners (say from neighbouring countries or from communities that are different from their own), they do not become agitated when others present points of view that are perhaps different from theirs—they respect the views of others. However, this does not mean that they necessarily agree with everything others have to say. They also have the right to question, undermine and refute the judgements of others. At least the possibility of learning is there when learners begin to scrutinise one another's views critically in an atmosphere of mutual respect for one another's different or at times conflicting judgements. When students show equal respect to one another, they are said to be critical, because criticality demands that we give due consideration to the views of others. In this way, learning to recognise different and often conflicting judgements of others seems to be a way in which to maximise Islamic education. This is so because critical learning has some connection with considering the merit of the conflicting views of others—that is, whether these views make sense, what MacIntyre (1990) refers to as taking others' views into 'systematic controversy'.

Secondly, to learn how to contribute to the justice of one's society and the world has some connection with a maximalist view of Islamic education. One cannot claim to be a critical learner if one's learning does not result in some form of action that has the potential to contribute to the achievement of democratic justice. I cannot imagine how *madrassah* learners can be critical if their learning does not cause them to act anew—they need to act with a sense of justice to others. Likewise, learners cannot be critical if their learning does not contribute to their advocating for a just world— for instance, the reduction of extreme and unacceptable levels of poverty on the African continent. This does not mean that they merely call for recognition of and respect for the rights of others (whether civil, political or social) within a critical learning agenda. Instead, they also stress the importance of taking responsibility for the rights of others—a matter of taking others' rights seriously or 'accepting appropriate responsibility for the rights of others, not just making a fuss about our own' (Callan, 1997: 73). For instance, people who champion the right to employment also consider as important the cause of others to take responsibility to meet the needs of those who are jobless. Such an understanding justice could potentially extend the mere recognition of, and respect for, others' rights to a position whereby we assume appropriate responsibility for the rights of others.

Thirdly, to learn what it means to be decent or civil (to be democratically just) has some connection to being critical—that is, virtuous. To show civility involves demonstrating what Macedo (1990) refers to as a sense of 'public-spiritedness'—that is, demonstrating a conscious awareness of others and recognising that they have to be respected on account of their difference. However, encountering one another's difference does not mean that one merely listens what others have to say without subjecting their truth claims to critical scrutiny. Critical learners also question one another's stories with the aim of gaining a deeper understanding of the texts of their lived experiences. I recall one learner who questioned another learner's bias towards Muslims in general. One learner claimed that Muslims are bigots, whereas another learner disagreed with this view on the basis that she lived in a Muslim country and her experience was that Muslims are generally moderate and respectful towards others (like herself) who have different cultural backgrounds. The point I am making is that questioning and undermining the views of others does not necessarily mean that one is disrespectful towards them. Rather, critically questioning people's unjustifiable assumptions about others is to treat them with honour—that is, not considering the unjustifiable views of others as beyond criticism. In this way, one demonstrates a sense of decency (civility)—one is democratically just and therefore critical.

In essence, when learners are taught about democratic justice, they learn to recognise equally the freedoms of others, to contribute to private and public justice, and to be decent. In this way, they learn to be 'happy' because happiness is linked to the realisation of a democratically just society on the grounds of having been exposed beforehand to texts which may enhance the possibility of achieving democratic justice.

What the aforementioned argument also foregrounds is the notion that happiness in this life—for Muslims in particular—is connected to the achievement of happiness in the afterlife. I want to raise an important point here about the belief of most Muslim suicide bombers that their violence against others would secure them a sojourn in the goodness of the hereafter. Such a view seems to be misplaced on the grounds of two reasons: firstly, if causing harm to others in this world is perceived as a legitimate claim to righteousness in the afterlife, then the argument does not hold because to do good in this world should be seen as an extension of good deeds in the afterlife. So, to blow up people because one wants to secure a place in paradise does not make sense if righteous and just conduct in the worldy life is inseparable from life in the hereafter; secondly, to embark upon suicide bombings for the sake of achieving one's own selfish ends also seems absurd for the reason that one invariably violates the freedom of others simply to be alive. Does one wish to determine the death of someone else who might not even wish to die as unexpectedly as suicide bombings often bring about? Thus, to strive for democratic justice could potentially deter possible aspirant suicide bombers from doing the unthinkable. And for this reason *madāris* ought to perpetuate the cultivation of democratic justice as an instance of true and legitimate happiness—a happiness to be enjoyed now which connects logically with possible happiness in the afterlife.

CHAPTER 5

Islamic education and cosmopolitanism

In the previous chapters I looked critically at three conceptions of Islamic education. I argued that conceptions of Islamic education ought to be considered as existing on a minimalist-maximalist continuum, meaning that the concepts associated with Islamic education do not have a single meaning, but that meanings are shaped depending on the minimalist and maximalist conditions which constitute them, that is, *tarbiyyah* (nurturing), *ta`lim* (learning) and *ta`dib* (goodness). I shall now explore some liberal conceptions of cosmopolitanism, showing how these notions connect with meanings of Islamic education. I particularly argue that maximalist views of Islamic education connect with cosmopolitanism, while minimalist views of Islamic education seem to undermine the pursuit of cosmopolitanism. This chapter builds on my previous arguments in defence of Islamic education for democratic citizenship. Before I develop the argument that the aforementioned conceptions of Islamic education can potentially enhance cosmopolitanism if implemented in a maximalist way, I first need to examine some interpretations of cosmopolitanism. I now turn my attention to this discussion.

Cosmopolitanism as education

Literature on cosmopolitanism abounds. In this section I focus on two interpretations of the concept. Some regard cosmopolitanism as a moral obligation one owes to every other person in the world without national or ethnic differentiation (Waldron, 2006: 83). Merry and De Ruyter (2009: 50) describe such a view of cosmopolitanism as the moral obligation one has towards strangers and not only those with whom one shares associative relations. For others, cosmopolitanism is about the many norms which define and sustain people's lives together; for instance, the principles that define human rights and crimes against humanity, the laws that govern refuge, asylum, travel and migration, and the rules shared by people—not just in any particular society, but all over the world (Benhabib, 2006: 13). Following the aforementioned interpretations of cosmopolitanism, one deduces that the concept is not just about the culture and moral sentiments that obligate people to act towards others in a certain way, but also the norms that govern or ought to govern their cooperative social relations—their reasoning together. When people reason together they exercise a virtue of caring which implies not only that one is being affectionate towards others, but also that one uses one's capability to cultivate in others the capacity to reach their own justifiable conclusions to which they can be held accountable. As a learner is taught the procedures of analysing concepts and the ways of finding construct meanings of concepts, and how she needs to articulate meanings skilfully, she has been initiated into a practice of evaluating, modifying and rejecting her judgements concerning analysing concepts. The learner is cared for if she has received good education about analysis and has acquired ways of discovering her own version of inquiry. In turn, the learner will act prudently, that is, exercise practical reasoning without just being told what to say and what to do. Simply put, the learner has been educated, that is, she has been taught to reason together with others. And, considering the view that cosmopolitanism also involves enacting norms such as those embedded in the virtue of caring, it follows that living cosmopolitanism is an educative experience. Hence, acting according to norms of cosmopolitanism is to practise education. The point I am making is that acting as a cosmopolitan is to act as an educated person—one who reasons together with others (such as being governed by the virtue of caring) in a strictly moral sense. It is for this reason that I concur with Merry and De Ruyter (2009: 52–54) when they explain cosmopolitanism as a moral obligation people have towards others whereby they recognise people's diverse ways of living and evoke a sense of care for their (people's) well-being, and work together to find pragmatic solutions that are suitable for everyone concerned. It seems as if Merry and De Ruyter (2009: 58)—like me—also consider cosmopolitanism to be fundamentally an educative activity because cosmopolitanism and education involve people who are morally obligated towards 'cultural others with the necessary pragmatist resolve to act on those obligations'.

What follows from the aforementioned is that education, in this instance Islamic education, cannot be disconnected from a notion of cosmopolitanism. Islamic education cannot be cosmopolitanism (and vice versa) if one of its constituent ideas is not that relations among human beings transcend the local interests of national identity and democratic boundaries. In contemporary society human relations—and in particular their forms of engagement—transcend individuals' national borders as they make claims beyond the thresholds of particular nationalities. They are 'citizens of the world' (Nussbaum, 1997) and their forms of engagement (education) are cosmopolitan—that is, they are governed by a moral obligation towards one another embedded in socially established norms of acceptable behaviour. This cosmopolitan engagement among people is corroborated by the following points of connection: recognition of human differences (Appiah, 2006), common humanity, that is, safeguarding human well-being and dignity (Dwyer, 2004), and shared moral norms of justice (Benhabib, 2006). Firstly, following Appiah (2006), people cannot be engaged in education if they do not develop respect for each other's differences. The mere fact that they engage with one another despite their differences is indicative of their educative relations—relations guided by the norms of respect for each other's differences. And if Islamic education does not lead to people connecting with one another on the grounds of respect for their differences, then there is no sense in cooperating and reasoning together. In this regard, the Qurān aptly states the following: 'O mankind! We have created you from a male and a female, and made you into nations and tribes, that you may know one another. Verily, the most honourable of you with Allāh is that (believer) who has At-Taqwa [i.e. he is one of the Muttaqūn (pious)]. Verily, Allāh is All-Knowing, All-Aware' (al-Hujurāt: 13). The point I am making is that Islamic education cannot be education if people do not engage with one another's differences—the very end of education is to establish opportunities for one to engage others in their otherness. Only if people engage one another through their differences might they have a real chance to connect with one another, to learn from one another and to respect one another. Some of my potential critics might find the view that Islamic education should be aimed at engaging others in their otherness rather odd. Jacques Derrida (1997: 17–18) believes that education has to do with connecting or relating to the other. Therefore, education is not some criterion or principle about which we can have knowledge beforehand and then set out to apply such knowledge (Biesta, 2001: 49). Rather, education 'is a concern for the otherness of the other' (Biesta, 2001: 48). Following this view of education, we cannot assume that Islamic education means this or that, for instance, treating learners equally or providing more assistance to underprivileged learners in the sense used by Rawls (1971). This would imply some prior knowledge of learners which one assumes would be useful in deciding what is 'right' for them. This is precisely the problem related to a minimalist view of Islamic education in some Islamic institutions in South Africa, which assumes that learners need to be taught to 'master' prescribed work on the basis of what is deemed good for them. The dilemma is that, since it has been decided well in advance what is good for learners, the possibility of learners coming to discover what is good for them seems to be ruled out. Their sense of inventiveness to reach out for unexpected possibilities seems to be disregarded—a matter of making education an 'impossibility', that is, what appears not to be possible (Biesta, 1998).

Education as a concern for the otherness of the other seems to have some affinity with a pedagogy of unknowing since both are crossed with what Zembylas (2005: 151) refers to as a responsiveness to the other which establishes opportunities that 'do not consider the learner as knowable and fixed'. 'Unknowability' implies that teachers are attentive to learners, that is, they 'encounter the unknowable mystery of the Other (which means) to *be* for the Other and attend to him/her…to *respond* to their students'. Therefore, having a concern for the unknowable Other—our learners— means that we have to 'experience' them; be 'vigilant to the Other' (Zembylas, 2005: 152). And, when we 'experience' learners, we hear and respond to them—a genuine aim of education. This is different from getting to 'know' your learners. Education, then, would not necessarily focus on acquiring knowledge, but would rather consider its practices as 'relations to otherness' (Zembylas, 2005: 153). In this sense, the way we engage with learners/the Other becomes a central concern for teaching— more specifically with regard to Islamic education. Education offers hope in 'opening up' the other (Zembylas, 2005: 156). Someone can receive information, but fail to engage actively with it—or, as Greene puts it, to reach out for meanings (1995: 57). In such a case a person cannot be said to be have been 'opened up', because learning requires of a person to construct meanings, to reach beyond where she is or to transcend the given (Greene, 1995: 111). And when a person has gone beyond the given, constructed meanings and found her own voice, she has been 'opened up'—she has acted with alertness. In other words, following Greene (1995: 34), people show an attentiveness to learning when they do not just look at themselves as passive receivers of information, but rather when they demonstrate a willingness 'to tell their stories, to pose their own questions, to be present—from their own perspectives—to the common world'. When a person becomes concerned with going beyond the given, she invariably wants to respond to other and different challenges that she might encounter. For example, a person who learns about the suffering of others imagines not only what others experience, but also how she might find ways to alleviate the vulnerabilities of others—to respond to others' suffering. In this way, being opened up involves wanting to look beyond the given and to search for meanings which would be responsive to the vulnerable experiences of others. Here I specifically think of many Muslim learners who claim to have learnt, yet do not even begin to wonder how their Islamic education could respond to—or as Greene (1995: 35) says, awaken in them a 'wide-awakeness' to—what must be done for those who remain tragically in need, who suffer deprivations such as family deterioration, neighbourhood decline, joblessness, illnesses such as HIV and AIDS, and addictions. These learners have not been 'opened up'—that is, ready to act justly and to respond to some of the conditions of those who might suffer vulnerabilities—to a maximalist view of Islamic education.

Secondly, following Dwyer (2004), a purpose of education is also for people to share commonalities; otherwise how would they experience what they possibly agree with? Cosmopolitanism allows space for different people to engage with one another's commonalities from which they could derive common understandings as they endeavour to contribute to shaping their societies. Often people's disagreements might end the conversation. However, they might have many things in common, but do not always consider them because their disagreements might be so stark. A cosmopolitan education demands that people engage with one another's commonalities and find ways in which they can collectively arrive at a decision—a situation which might possibly strengthen their relations despite their differences. Engaging one another's commonalities provides participants in some way with opportunities (teachers) to cultivate in others (learners) the ability to listen to what others have to say (fellow-learners); no matter how ill-informed or unimportant the points of view seem to be. The point about listening to others is that it has some connection to understanding others' reasons. Without listening to others we cannot begin to comprehend the kinds of reasons for their actions that might be intelligible to us; that would enable us to respond to them in ways that they too might find intelligible (MacIntyre, 1999: 14). In other words, we can only understand others and respond to them in ways which could be intelligible if we could justify to others why we find their reasons 'reasonable' or not. In this way, listening to others could contribute to deliberative action. The point I am making is that in the first place listening to others involves 'standing back' or detaching oneself from one's reasons and asking if others' reasons are in fact justifiable or not. Here one moves away from merely listening to others towards being able to evaluate others' reasons. And when one evaluates others' reasons (through listening) one would invariably set out to revise one's own or abandon them or replace them with other reasons (MacIntyre, 1999: 91)—what Burbules (1993: 5) refers to as 'the capacity to *admit* (to oneself and to others) that one is wrong...our capacity to hear and respond thoughtfully to the criticisms of others'. In this way, one not only becomes a good listener, but also deliberative in the sense that one detaches oneself from one's own reasons to revise or abandon them in the light of what others (to whom one listens and with whom one engages) have to offer. MacIntyre (1999: 96) argues that we come to know when we are able not just to evaluate our reasons as better or worse, but also when we detach ourselves from the immediacy of our own desires in order to 'imagine alternative realistic futures' through engaging collegially (deliberatively)—I would say, listening to what others have to say. Phillion (2002: 548) makes a similar point about listening being an important aspect of 'narrative inquiry'—that is, to always ask why something is done rather than rushing to judge the learners' actions. Garrison (1996) makes the point that active listening involves being 'vulnerable to the other'—a matter of engaging them with what they have in common with one.

Thirdly, following Benhabib's elucidation of cosmopolitanism (2006), and the link I have established with cosmopolitanism and education thus far, education cannot be disconnected from the need to ensure that people attend justly to the moral concerns of others. Benhabib posits the following:

> Every person, and every moral agent, who has interest and whom my actions and consequences of my actions can impact and affect in some manner or another is potentially a moral conversation partner with me: I have a moral obligation to *justify my action with reasons* to this individual or to the representative of this being.

We are all potentially participants in such conversations of justification (Benhabib, 2006: 18; emphasis in the original).

What Benhabib (2006) clearly advocates is a Kantian notion of hospitality towards the other. This implies that other people should always be included in the conversation and not be treated as if they are aliens, strangers or illegal immigrants. This view of hospitality further extends to considering the vulnerabilities of people and acting hospitably (compassionately) towards them. Only then do people have a real chance to build relationships. Central to this kind of cosmopolitanism is the equal regard one should have for all peoples. That is, justice should be desired for all individuals or groups.

In essence, Islamic education should always be connected to people engaging one another's commonalities and differences, and to the moral concern that justice for all peoples ought to shape our relations. Now that I have given an account of cosmopolitanism in relation to education, I shall examine whether an understanding of Islamic education can and should make possible the cultivation of cosmopolitanism.

Cosmopolitanism as an instance of Islamic education

Thus far I have argued that education cannot be delinked from cosmopolitanism, neither can cosmopolitanism be viewed independently from education. These two ideas are intertwined on the grounds that both concepts are grounded in a moral obligation people have for one another, and that both are guided by norms of acceptable, cooperative human social relations. And, if Islamic education is a form of education its meanings cannot be dissociated from what an education for cosmopolitanism means. The point I am making is that a maximalist view of Islamic education ought to involve the cultivation of cosmopolitanism; otherwise its link with education would not be at all defensible. Education and cosmopolitanism are determined in the first place by moral sentiments and norms of shared human activity. And if Islamic education involves the engagement of people with the aim of finding peaceful human co-existence, I cannot imagine Islamic education not being shaped by moral sentiments and norms of human co-existence and reasoning together.

I now turn to a discussion of Islamic education and their implications for cosmopolitanism. A minimalist view of *ta`dib* (goodness) considers the purpose of education as biased towards the Muslim community. This means that Muslims patriotically and at times blindly support other Muslims, because it is narrowly conceived that goodness is only meant for those of an Islamic orientation—Muslims are the only ones who will eventually enjoy the permanent bliss of paradise, for example. This account of education (in a minimalist sense) is connected with a narrow view that the Muslim community should be prejudiced in favour of any other person.[1] A maximalist account of *ta`dib* (goodness) considers every individual, irrespective of linguistic, cultural, religious, socio-economic, political and ethnic differences, as worthy of respect as a person. More specifically, such a view of Islamic education demands justice for all people and holds that the ownership of goodness is not the reserved property of any single group of persons, whether Muslim or non-Muslim. Goodness is for society and not Muslims alone, and every person should be a candidate for being a representative of goodness on the basis of the acts of justice she performs. Now that I have given an exposition of what a minimalist-maximalist account of Islamic education entails, I shall move on to an exploration of how a maximalist interpretation of Islamic education can cultivate cosmopolitan ideals.

With reference to rearing, learning and goodness, a minimalist view of Islamic education does undoubtedly not favour the cultivation of cosmopolitanism. Firstly, if the uncritical acceptance of views is considered to be important for Muslims, then it is very unlikely that others' views will be considered to be equally important. Secondly, an overemphasis on learning by rote would not necessarily contribute to enhancing deliberation about issues relevant to the Islamic faith and society in general. I cannot imagine how liberal thinkers would consider medieval jurists' views on the advancement of democratic education, for instance, on an equal basis, I also cannot see why less importance should be given to the established traditions of liberal conceptions of democratic education. Unless, of course, medieval juristic views are allowed to be interpreted and adapted to the democratic concerns of, say, Islamic schools. The whole idea of not subjecting your views to critical scrutiny by others who in turn can give a justifiable account of their reasons, and vice versa, is incommensurate with the idea of democratic deliberative engagement. Thirdly, privileging the Muslim community only, as if justice cannot be wished for anybody else, is an idea that is out of line with cosmopolitanism for the reason that cosmopolitanism demands a moral obligation towards all people, whoever they may be. If justice is considered to be important for Muslims only and others are regarded as not equally important, it would virtually become impossible for cosmopolitanism to be cultivated. Hence, education would become *un*educational. Firstly, the point about respecting people for who they are suggests that one recognises that persons are capable of reflecting on their desires, setting their own ends, and rationally pursuing some means to an end, by allowing them space and opportunity and even by aiding them in their pursuit to some extent, provided their means and ends are based on respect for others. Secondly, people respect others as moral agents when they recognise others to reciprocate the moral standing they have attributed to others, that is, they recognise that others should not be written off as creatures who can only respond to power, bribery and manipulation. Thirdly, respect for people involves considering them as particular individuals, whose identities are bound up with particular projects, personal attachments, and traditions. In the fourth place, to respect is also to criticise if necessary; and finally, to respect means to appreciate the different values others have found in their groups (Hill, 2000: 77–80). Thus, in a cosmopolitan society, if people are not recognised for having something worthwhile to say (that is, rationally), or are excluded on account of their difference, or are allowed to get away with unsubstantiated claims without being criticised or taken into systematic controversy, 'respect for persons' would no longer exist and by implication any deliberation would be short-lived.

A maximalist account of Islamic education contains most of the constitutive features that connect Islamic education with the cultivation of cosmopolitanism. An Islamic education that recognises the otherness of others (both their commonalities and differences) and strives to achieve justice for all through processes of deliberation is consonant with some of the ideals of cosmopolitanism. Similarly, an Islamic education that engenders compassion towards vulnerable others, irrespective of their religious identities, will go far in advancing cosmopolitan ideals. My potential critics might argue that cosmopolitanism might undermine the very ideals of deliberation through its insistence on recognising the diverse ways of others, including others' right to freedom of speech, for instance. Consider some of the vehement attacks waged against the morality of the Muslim community through insults directed at Islam's Prophet Muhammad

(SAW). The cosmopolitan argument is not that freedom of speech should be constrained, but rather that freedom of speech that has the potential to cause an injustice to others should be constrained. This is not a denial of the cosmopolitan ideal of freedom of expression. Instead, freedom of expression ought to be curtailed if it leads to an injustice towards others (Gutmann, 2003). What (Gutmann, 1996: 70) argues for is that education should encourage citizens to deliberate about justice for the fellow citizens as well as their fellow human beings—an idea of democratic humanism that is not incommensurate with cosmopolitanism. If freedom of speech is not constrained by the need to avoid injustice towards others, the possibility for deliberation and respect for persons, irrespective of their differences, will in any case dissipate.

An Islamic education that does not hold the promise of cultivating cosmopolitanism has the potential of breeding intolerance, disrespect and even antagonism towards others. If an Islamic education is only meant to socialise people with dogma and blind patriotism towards the Muslim community, the possibility arises for isolation and confrontation of significant proportions. Of course, confrontation does not mean that people would and should necessarily inflict harm on one another. In fact, deliberation has a meaningful chance of achieving its desired aims. But then Islamic education should also create opportunities for people to take risks as they endeavour to achieve the unimagined or unthinkable; otherwise the end of education would already have been achieved. Moreover, taking risks would evoke in people the capacity to confront one another through deliberation. And, as has been argued for previously, deliberation happens when no one has the right to silence dissent and where participants can speak their minds. And when people (teachers and learners) can speak their minds, they are also prepared to take risks which would place them favourably with respect to doing justice to their society. Teachers and learners who are prepared to challenge forms of injustice such as poverty, racism and xenophobia in their society do so for the sake of cultivating cosmopolitan justice—they act as cosmopolitans willing to take the risk of speaking their minds as they enact their hospitality. Taking risks as cosmopolitans does not merely call for recognition and respect of other's rights (whether civil, political or social), but also for taking responsibility for the rights of others. Acting responsibly as cosmopolitans would instil in teachers and learners qualities which can help to build a better society—one free from social oppression, economic marginalisation and subtle forms of racist exclusion. The point is that unless Islamic educational institutions such as *madāris* become havens of cosmopolitanism aimed at producing a better future for all people, Islamic education would not have seriously engaged with challenges of the unexpected.

This brings me to a discussion on what Islamic educational institutions in particular ought to teach in order to advance cosmopolitanism. Firstly, Muslim teachers should constantly inculcate in learners the important virtues of cosmopolitanism in order to prevent the possibility of injustices against human beings. The possibility that inhumane and unjust acts against human beings can be reduced is highly likely if learners are educated to be cosmopolitan in outlook. What does this entail? Important virtues of cosmopolitanism include, firstly, the capacity to deliberate as free and equal citizens in a democratic polity, and secondly, conducting such deliberations in such a way that they are about the demands of justice for all individuals (Gutmann, 1996: 68–69). If we deliberate as free and equal citizens, then we first of all give an account of what we do to others, who might find our reasons justifiable or not. In turn, we consider the reasons of others equally, which can lead either to our accepting or rejecting their reasons, or to their understanding of our reasons or justifications. Such justifications and concomitant actions arise in an atmosphere of free and open expression, and are hindered when our reasons embody injustice towards others. Educating Muslim learners to be cosmopolitan citizens involves inculcating in them a spirit of openness to, and respect for, the justifications of others; a recognition that others should be listened to, and that injustices should not be done to others under the guise of equal and free expression. In fact, cosmopolitanism is connected to what Benhabib (2006: 48) refers to as participating in democratic iterations—those linguistic, legal, cultural and political repetitions-in-transformation. A democratic iteration is characterised by acts of reappropriation and reinterpretation. One simply has to engage in an unending debate with others through democratic self-reflection and self-determination and public defensiveness. It is a profound sense of democratic reflexivity which appeals to recursive questioning and reiterated justifications. For instance, consider the 'scarf affair' (the example that Benhabib uses to expound on democratic reiterations) in France in 1989, which started with the expulsion from their school of three scarf-wearing Muslim girls. Seven years later there was a mass exclusion of twenty-three

Muslim girls from their school. Confrontations between school authorities and young Muslim girls and women continued throughout the 1990s and well into the 21ˢᵗ. century. The intervention of the French authorities to ban the wearing of the veil in the schools at first seemed like an attempt of a progressive state bureaucracy to modernise what appeared to be 'backward' customs of a group. However, this intervention cascaded into a series of democratic iterations: from the intense debate among the French public about the meaning of wearing the scarf, to the self-defence of the girls involved and the re-articulation of the meaning of their actions, to the encouragement of other immigrant women to wear their headscarves to the workplace. Basically, women have learned to 'talk back (to the state)—a matter of engaging and contesting the meanings of the Islamic practices they want to uphold. To my mind, democratic iteration is precisely what we require in Islamic institutions to make sure that the education system we now have to implement has been subjected to democratic reflexivity and recursive justifications, which means listening to the views of those involved in the implementation of the curriculum and then to 'talk back'.

Secondly, if cosmopolitanism demands that people deliberate about the demands of justice for all individuals then, as aptly put by Gutmann (1996: 69), 'doing what is right' cannot be reduced to loyalty to, or identification with, any existing group of human beings. Islamic educational institutions 'should teach learners, on the one hand, about their duties as citizens to advance justice and not to limit performance of these duties to some individuals or groups, and on the other hand, about their responsibilities as citizens to support institutional ways of moving towards better societies and a better world' (Gutmann, 1996: 71). Like Callan (1999: 198), I contend that learners should be taught 'to see their neighborhoods and the international community as arenas of civic participation'.

Thirdly, learners should be taught not to condone the perpetration of crimes against humanity. When one cultivates such a norm of cosmopolitanism, learners are taught not to ignore the right to temporary residence of strangers who come to one's country. In her words, 'to refuse sojourn to victims of religious wars, to victims of piracy or ship-wreckage when such refusal would lead to their demise, is untenable' (Benhabib, 2006: 22). Put sharply, cosmopolitanism expressly prohibits crimes against humanity—that is, it does not permit government officials, state bureaucrats and others in positions of power to act in such a way as to allow murder, extermination, enslavement, deportation and other inhumane acts (genocide, ethnocide, mass expulsions, rape and forced labour) to be committed against any civilian population before or during war; nor does it allow persecution on political, racial or religious grounds. Certainly in some parts of the world a cosmopolitan education becomes a necessity because of the political, racial and religious persecution of some communities. And, to cultivate the virtue of respecting the dignity of all human beings is to enact an Islamic education for cosmopolitanism. In essence, educating for cosmopolitanism does not only involve cultivating in people a sense of deliberating together freely and equally about their common and collective destiny; it is also about achieving justice for all. Deliberating about the demands of justice is a central virtue of cosmopolitanism, because it is primarily (but not exclusively) through our empowerment of cosmopolitan citizens that we can further the cause of justice around the world. This brings me to a discussion of some of the limitations of cosmopolitanism in relation to Islamic education.

The aforementioned elucidation of cosmopolitan seems to set up peace as an elitist agenda of a maximalist view of Islamic education. In what follows I argue that forgiveness (*tawbah*) ought to be linked to the advancement of a cosmopolitan ideal of Islamic education. Why? The Qurān is replete with verses that advance the notion of forgiveness. Therefore, any maximalist conception of Islamic education cannot be connected with cosmopolitanism without being attentive to the notion of forgiveness. The Qurān states the following about forgiveness: 'And whoever does evil or wrongs himself but afterwards seeks Allāh's Forgiveness, he will find Allāh Oft-Forgiving, Most Merciful' (*al- Nisā* 110). But should forgiveness be limited to pardoning what is forgivable? This seems to be an issue on which cosmopolitanism appears to be muted and which I intend to explore in order to make a case for a maximalist view of Islamic education more plausible. Derrida (1997: 33) argues for a view of forgiveness which builds on the premise 'that forgiveness must announce itself as impossibility itself...(and that) it can only be possible in doing the impossible'. For Derrida (1997: 33), 'doing the impossible' implies forgiving the 'unforgivable'. In his words, 'forgiveness forgives only the unforgivable'—that is, atrocious and monstrous crimes against humanity which might not be conceived as possible to forgive (Derrida 1997: 32). Derrida (1997: 44) explicates forgiveness as 'a gracious gift without exchange and without condition'. Amongst crimes against humanity Derrida (1997: 52) includes genocide (say of Hutus against Tutsis), torture and terrorism. This notion of forgiving the 'unforgivable' is spawned by the view that forgiveness is an act without finality—that is, the guilty (the one who perpetrates the evil) is considered as being capable of repeating the crime without repentance or promise that he or she will be transformed. And, forgiving the 'unforgivable' takes into consideration that the crime might be repeated, which makes forgiveness an act (of madness) of the impossible (Derrida, 1997: 45). Now a maximalist account of forgiveness that makes possible the act of forgiving the 'unforgivable' makes sense, because if Tutsis are not going to venture into forgiving the 'unforgivable' genocidal acts of Hutus, these two different tribal communities on the African continent might not begin to connect with one another and a process of inducing transformation within a Congolese or Rwandan society might not begin to take place. Similarly, if Bosnian Muslims are not going to forgive their Serbian oppressors, the likelihood of cosmopolitanism seems far away. Such a Derridian view of forgiveness is grounded in an understanding that 'nothing is impardonable' (Derrida, 1997: 47) and, that 'grand beginnings' are often celebrated and redirected through amnesia of the most atrocious happenings—a point in case is South Africa's democracy which grew out of forgiving those 'unforgivable' racial bigots who committed heinous crimes against those who opposed the racist state.

Of course, I am adamant about the prospects for a maximalist view of Islamic education *through* peace—that is, imagining and creating spaces where forgiveness, healing and engagement might actually be made possible. But here, I want to invoke the potential that violence has to offer (somewhat paradoxically) to cosmopolitanism. Following Arendt's (1969) analysis, 'temporary' violence can be considered to be a phenomenon whereby people impose themselves on others, thus making others the 'instruments' of their will (Arendt, 1969: 56). In other words, violence is an instrumental means of coercion (Arendt, 1969: 44). So, in Rwanda and Congo, Hutu militia murder, torture, rape and maim Tutsi women and children because they use such instrumental acts in order to terrorise Tutsis. Off course, non-violence can counteract violence because unlike violence, non-violence is capable of speech acts—that is, 'violence itself is incapable of speech, and not merely that speech is helpless when confronted with violence' (Arendt, 1963: 19). Unlike violence, which is determined by silence (Arendt, 1969: 77), such as the silence of both victims and perpetrators of torture in Nazi concentration camps, non-violence draws on the authoritative voice of speech. It is here that non-violence can begin to tackle the Rwandan/Congolese genocide. Like Arendt, I contend that there is no legitimate justification for violence and that the use of violence will only result in more violence. Yet, following Cavell (1979) and Arendt (1963), we sometimes require a disruption of existing practices of violence through 'temporary' violence. Is it conceivable that non-violent resistance will always be met with non-terrorisation and peace? I do not imagine so. If Hutu militia were to be resisted non-violently, massacre and submission of Tutsis would be the order of the day. Thus, in a Cavellian sense, we require a momentary breakage from non-violence in order to ensure lasting change in Rwanda and the Congo—that is, a condition ought to be set up whereby speech could become dominant in an attempt to resolve conflict. What this argument amounts to, is that non-violence with its insistence on speech acts can temporarily create conditions for violence to counteract the destructive force of more violence.

Thus, if a maximalist view of (cosmopolitan) Islamic education could be extended to forgiving the unforgivable and to the temporary use of violence, new openings for education and new encounters with otherness might be a distinct possibility. Would it not be in the interest of world peace if Palestinians would forgive Israelis and vice versa? In the context of a maximalist view of Islamic education, what this argument suggests is that new openings in curriculum would be possible only if new encounters with otherness are considered and actually pursued. Islamic education can only gain if we begin to take up a renewed interest in the cosmopolitan tradition of education—a cosmopolitan view of education which does not take us 'nowhere or everywhere' (as its critiques would like to propound) but indeed 'somewhere'. And, certainly in society today Islamic education ought to counteract the kinds of inhospitalities and inhumaneness which have become so pervasive in our institutions. Papastephanou (2002: 69) aptly expresses this call for cosmopolitan education as follows: 'Cosmopolitanism envisions peace and reconciliation…(which) paves paths for encounters. Encounters undo identities, reshuffle their interpretative material and their self-understanding, and unleash new creative energies.' In fact, a cosmopolitan Islamic education (a maximalist view) encourages one to engage imaginatively with respect to yet-to-come possibilities that might encourage the advent of society in a new image grounded in equality, compassion and care—it must embrace this futurity in the now, in which the past is also present, and reverberates (Quinn, 2010: 24).

NOTES

[1]   I am not suggesting that Muslims should not patriotically support other Muslims. However, if Muslims are wrong, one cannot blindly support their actions. (Of course, even if Muslims are not wrong, 'blind' following would be unwise.) For instance, if Muslims are responsible for terrorist acts, these acts should be condemned.

CHAPTER 6

Towards a *madrassah* imaginary: Cultivating a maximalist view of Islamic education

Thus far, I have argued that Islamic education has the best chance of achieving its maximalist ideals if framed along the lines of democratic iterations and deliberations, compassionate imagining and cosmopolitanism. In fact, the prospect for world peace, reconciliation and forgiveness might become a real possibility. In this chapter I shall offer an imaginary perspective of what I think a *madrassah* ought to look like if it hopes to extend the maximalist understandings of Islamic education for which I have argued hitherto.

I have argued that enacting democratic iterations and cultivating cosmopolitan hospitality might offer oneself and others a better opportunity to learn. What democratic iterations and cosmopolitan hospitality have in mind is to create conditions whereby genuine Islamic learning can take place and where one would learn to experience the other. In such an environment there would no longer be a possibility for violence, aggression and the ridicule of the other. But then one learns to take responsibility for the other. It is this practice of assuming responsibility for the other through Islamic learning which I now wish to pursue in order to find out how one's relationship with the other could potentially be enhanced. For this discussion I turn to the seminal thoughts of Jacques Derrida.

Islamic education as responsibility for the other

Derrida (2001) maintains that it is the responsibility of educational institutions (such as the modern university), and I would argue *madāris* as well, to be 'unconditional', by which he means that it should have the freedom to assert, question and profess. In other words, for Derrida (2001) the future of the profession of academics is determined by 'the university without conditions'. Put differently, Derrida frames the profession of those academics who work at the university as a responsibility. This responsibility to profess is no longer associated with a profession of faith, a vow or promise, but rather an engagement: 'to profess is to offer a guide in the course of engaging one's responsibility' (Derrida, 2001: 35). So, an unconditional university is one that enacts its responsibility of engagement. And if learning is one of the practices associated with that of a university and a *madrassah*, learning *per se* should also be about enacting a responsibility. Derrida connects the idea of responsibility to the university, but I now specifically want to make an argument for learning in *madāris* along the lines of his conception of responsibility. This is not to say that he does not link responsibility to learning, but rather I want to make the argument for responsibility as a corollary of learning in a more nuanced way than Derrida seemingly does.

From my reading of Derrida's idea of responsibility I infer three features which are central to what could underscore learning: responsibility means to engage the other freely, openly and critically; to act responsibly is to hold open a space for non-instrumental thinking; and to be responsible is to constantly resist or disrupt practices which move towards completion (Derrida, 2001: 35–36). What are the implications of responsible action for Islamic learning in *madāris*? Firstly, a responsible Muslim learner (one who has learnt) concerns himself or herself with social problems. Responsible learners endeavour to argue openly, freely and critically with others in an attempt to solve social problems. Such a form of learning provides a sphere in which genuine critical discourse (investigation and debate as against mere textbook transmission) takes place, and at the same time is likely to produce activities of 'value' in addressing societal problems. In this way Muslim learners are taught to be critically reflective about society and can simultaneously contribute to the achievement of, say, improved nutrition and health services, more secure livelihoods, and security against crime and physical violence. In a way, responsible Muslim learners are responsible citizens who are intellectually, culturally and technologically adept at and committed to addressing social problems.

Secondly, for a responsible Muslim learner to attend to non-instrumental thinking means that such a learner does not merely perform his or her responsibility for the sake of something else, for instance, for physical needs, reputation and gratitude. Such instrumental actions would render responsibility conditional. Responsible learners are concerned with the intrinsic worth of their actions (and not with the convenient applications of their learning) and they are engaged in just, autonomous, non-instrumental activities. Such learners' actions are not rooted in dubious motives and/or interests. Here I agree with Haverhals (2007: 4250), who claims that such learners would enhance 'the development of personal autonomy, which also has a public significance'. The public roles of such learners and the educative value of their activities are affected by a legitimate concern to act responsibly.

Thirdly, a responsible Muslim learner constantly disrupts or resists the possibility that knowledge production has moved towards or attained completion. Such irresponsible actions would ignore the contingency and unpredictability of actions themselves. A responsible Muslim learner always strives to embark on new narratives in the making, or perhaps moves towards some unimagined possibility. And for this, responsible Muslim learners constantly think of themselves as projects in the making—their work cannot attain completion and perfection. There is always something more to learn which, of course, brings me to how one can potentially respond as a responsible learner to the dilemmas that confront Muslims. These dilemmas involve the reluctance of many Muslims to engage others (of non-Muslim faith perhaps) deliberatively and iteratively; the seeming unwillingness to attend to one another in a hospitable way, as is evident from the violent moments that have become endemic to many African communities, particularly in Nigeria where the destruction of mosques and churches has become prevalent in societal life. Acting as a responsible Muslim learner means that one constantly disrupts the practices which one embarks on in pursuit of cultivating non-violence, tolerance and respect for persons.

I shall now illustrate what I mean by constantly disrupting the practices one can embark on in order to combat some of the societal and political ills. For this discussion I have chosen the example of the troops from Guinea who are being accused of raping several thousands of women. A salient question arises here: What can a responsible Muslim learner do to challenge such an inhumane atrocity—how can he or she disrupt such an inhumane practice? In the first place, a responsible Muslim learner acts by giving an account of his or her actions. That is, they have to be answerable for their actions, in this instance, the act of doing or not doing something about the rape of women in Guinea. They can either vociferously condemn the heinous crimes perpetrated against women or remain silent about the incident. They might remain silent because they fear reprisals by some members of the military or because they ignore the international community's calls to speak out. Be that as it may, actually doing something such as offering reasons or being silent about the situation involves giving an account of oneself and one's reasons. In my view a preferred accountable action would be to condemn the crime of rape perpetrated against helpless women. Secondly, acting as a responsible Muslim learner involves mustering the support of others who themselves stand up against crimes that violate human dignity. Thirdly, and most importantly, being a responsible Muslim learner actually involves doing something about rectifying the situation—that is, doing something to change the situation by causing a sudden disruption. This could include a range of actions such as campaigning widely for the war to stop in Guinea or for an international tribunal to put the military junta on trial. Hence, acting as a responsible Muslim learner involves identifying a wrong and actually doing something about changing that wrong. The point I am making is that if Islamic learning does not lead to actions which can alleviate, quell or even eradicate societal and political injustices, then such learning is not constituted by responsibility. I would like to believe that all forms of Islamic learning should be guided by an ethical element—one that involves combating or disrupting various forms of injustice.

Certainly on the African continent, Islamic learning has to be connected with the achievement of justice for all. Only then can learning be of value in leading to human flourishing. This makes sense considering that too many injustices are perpetrated by Africans against Africans. And if Africa has any chance of prospering economically, culturally and politically, the emphasis in all educational institutions (including *madāris*) should be on cultivating a conception of learning that can engender in people a willingness to deliberate in iterative fashion (learning that encourages talking back), an attentiveness to connect hospitably with others, and finally, to act responsibly with the aim of changing a bad situation. Connecting learning with such cosmopolitan virtues would go some way towards attending to Africa's and the world's moral problems—problems to which the world and certainly Muslim teachers should not be turning a blind eye.

Thus, learning through democratic iterations, the exercise of cosmopolitan hospitality, and the enactment of one's responsibility towards the other would certainly enhance the pursuit of genuine Islamic education in *madāris*. This is so for the reason that 'learning to talk back', performing hospitable actions, and enacting one's responsibility towards others are deeply reflexive and inconclusive practices—those qualities reminiscent of maximalist forms of Islamic education through which people are continuously and actively engaged in acts of meaning making.

Islamic education as critique: Reconstituting the place of thinking in the *madrassah*

What does reconstituting the place of thinking (*tafakkur*) mean? But first, I need to point out the importance of thinking in Islamic education before exploring how a Derridian notion of thinking can possibly be used to reconstitute the place of reason in *madāris*. In the Qurān (*al-Nahl*: 44), the Prophet Muhammad (SAW) is described as the expounder of Qurānic guidance: 'And We have sent down unto thee (also) the Message; that thou Mayest explain clearly to [wo]men what is sent for them, and that they may give thought [*tafakkur*]'. This verse makes it clear that Qurānic guidance is not just a matter of unquestioning acceptance, but also of thinking (*tafakkur*), that notion which creates space for questioning and challenging. Again, in the Qurān (*al-Jāthiyah*: 13), knowledge is connected to the verb *tafakkara*: 'And He has made subservient to you, [as a gift] from Himself, all that is in the heavens and on earth: in this, behold, there are messages for people who think.' This verse exhorts people to embark on *tafakkur*, that is, the ability to reflect, to think, in pursuit of understanding the messages (*āyāt*) of Allāh. Moreover, thinking is also confirmed through other Qurānic concepts such as *fiqh* and *ilm*. The Qurān (*al-Anā`m*: 98) links messages (*āyāt*) of Allāh with the verb *faqiha*: 'And He is it who has brought you (all) into being out of one living entity, and (has appointed for each of you) a time-limit (on earth) and a resting-place (after death): clearly, indeed, have We spelled these messages (*āyāt*) unto people who can grasp the truth (*yafqahūn*, which is derived from *faqiha*, i.e. to think about truth)'. It is not surprising to note that Sahīh al-Bukhāri mentions a *Hadīth* which considers those who use *faqiha* (thinking) as having gained the bounty of Allāh: 'If Allāh wants to do good to a person, he makes him comprehend (*yufaqqah*, which is derived from *faqiha*) the religion, more specifically Islamic education. Likewise, the Qurān is replete with verses which link messages

(*āyāt*) of Allāh to *ya`lamūn* (*al-Baqra:* 164 *Āli* al-Imrān: 118; *al-Akhzāb:* 32)—
a concept which is derived from `alima (to think).

Following Derrida, firstly, thinking holds that 'reason must be rendered' (Derrida 2004: 136). Literally, thinking means to explain or account for something, that is, to ground, justify, motivate, authorise. Only then, a reason is said to be rendered. So, if a Muslim teacher can justify her association with a particular action, she thinks because of rendering a reason for action. For instance, if a Muslim teacher can justify why she aligns herself with a maximalist view of Islamic education, such a teacher is thinking because she renders a reason (by which others might be persuaded or not) in defence of the view of the Islamic education she embarks on. Following such an account of thinking, if a Muslim teacher does not pledge in advance a *madrassah's* association with a maximalist view of Islamic education for some utilitarian purpose, but rather renders a reason or reasons for its epistemological journey, she functions within the parameters of a community of thinking—that is, she leaves open the possibility of grounding a *madrassah's* course of action. Often *madāris* in South Africa too readily reveal their plans for action to indicate their public good orientation. Yet, a *madrassah* seldom justifies why it prefers to embark on a particular form of action. Put differently, such a *madrassah* too often displays its intended utilitarian ends without rendering a justifiable reason for its actions. If a Muslim teacher could motivate her *madrassah's* commitment to an emancipatory pedagogy on the grounds that such a pedagogy would establish opportunities for deliberative engagement, unhindered freedom, and equitable change, then such a Muslim teacher can be associated with a community of thinking. On the contrary, if the aims for this pedagogy are geared towards excessive fundraising for the Islamic institution's future plans, then such a *madrassah* cannot be said to align itself with the work of a community of thinking that always programmes its actions in view of utility. In the words of Derrida (2004: 148, 150), 'this thinking must…prepare students to take new analyses' and 'to transform the modes of writing, the pedagogic scene, the procedures of academic exchange, the relation to languages, to other disciplines, to the institution in general, to its inside and its outside'. Certainly, for the plausible pursuit of Islamic education in a maximalist way this makes a lot of sense, considering that many of the practices at *madāris* might often engender uncriticality and mediocrity which reflect a serious lack of conceptual clarity and epistemological authority.

Secondly, a 'community of thinking' would go beyond the 'profound and the radical' (Derrida, 2004: 153). The enactment of such thinking is 'always risky; it always risks the worst' (Derrida, 2004: 153). A community of thinking that goes 'beyond' with the intention of taking more risks would become more attentive to unimagined possibilities, unexpected encounters, and perhaps the lucky find. Nothing is impossible because it opens the institution not only 'to the outside and the bottomless, but also…to any sort of interest' (Derrida, 2004: 153). Certainly in South Africa, where the moral fabric of post-apartheid society is withering away, *madāris* require thoughtful, highly inspired and risky Islamic educational contributions that can address issues of racism, gender inequality, patriarchy, domestic violence and the HIV and AIDS pandemic. Risky efforts would enhance the possibility of highly contemplative and theoretical contributions that go beyond practical usefulness and provide us with more to know than any other (Derrida 2004: 130). I am thinking in particular of the need for risky intellectual contributions in cosmopolitanism, which might address the sporadic xenophobic outbursts in South Africa. Nowadays, too few Muslim teachers are prepared to take risks and to move beyond what already exists. Here I propose that teachers learn to substantiate claims and propositions— only in doing so they can begin to think of taking more risks. The point is that they don't consider taking risks because they seem to be obsessed with producing work aimed at what works mechanically.

Thirdly, I agree with Derrida that an educational institution is 'supposed to *represent* society. And in a certain way it has done so: it has reproduced society's scenography, its views, conflicts, contradictions, its play and its differences, and also its desire for organic union in a total body' (Derrida, 2004: 154). In Derridian fashion, the 'organic language' which used to be associated with *madāris* prior to 1994 happened to *reflect* apartheid society—excessive rote learning, lack of critical engagement and political complacency. That is, its discourses seemed to have countenanced pluralism and democracy. But when a *madrassah represents* society then reflection is also given to another form of thinking—one which is provocative and which guides the institution to act accountably and responsibly (Derrida, 2004: 154). Derrida refers to this form of thinking as an 'etymological wink' or 'twinkling of thinking' which calls on the educational institution to act with 'renewal' during a period of decadence. This implies that a *madrassah* has an instantaneous 'desire for memory and exposure to the future'. Put differently, a *madrassah* uses its knowledge discourses to pursue truth(s), yet at the same time uses its truthful knowledges to contribute to a 'renewal' of society's decadent situations—whether they be physical, moral, cultural, political and/or economic. This form of thinking opens up a *madrassah* to 'chance', that is, what a society does not have and what is not yet.

A thinking that demands that reasons are rendered, encourages risk taking, and contributes to renewal is appropriately referred to by Derrida as 'critique' (Derrida, 2004: 162). As for Derrida, so for me critique is a form of dissonance and questioning which is not dominated and intimidated by the power of performativity: 'This thinking must also unmask—an infinite task—all the ruses of end-orienting reason, the paths by which apparently disinterested research can find itself indirectly reappropriated, reinvested by programs of all sorts' (Derrida, 2004: 148). This basically entails always asking: 'What is at stake (in technology, the sciences, production and productivity)?' It allows us to take more risks, to deal openly with the radical incommensurability of the language games that constitute our society, and invites new possibilities to emerge. Critique is a matter of enhancing the possibility of dissent and diversity of interpretations (Burik, 2009: 301); of complicating what is taken for granted, pointing to what has been overlooked in establishing identities (Burik, 2009: 302); an active opening up of one's own thought structures that is necessary for other ways to find an entrance (Burik, 2009: 304). Put differently: it is performing a kind of thinking innately concerned with creating possibilities for dissent, diversity of interpretations, complicating the taken-for-granted and opening up to the other.

Islamic education and friendship

Thus far I have made an argument for a maximalist view of Islamic education through assuming responsibility for the other, and by reconstituting the place of thinking in *madāris*. In the last part of this chapter I shall show how both Sherman's (1997) and Derrida's (1997) ideas of friendship can be used to nurture maximalist forms of teaching and learning which involve taking risks in *madāris*. My argument in defence of taking risks through friendships is hopefully a move away from fostering deliberative democratic interactions among teachers and learners that could potentially ignore forms of action that involve challenging, undermining and disagreeing with one's friends.

Sherman's (1997) account of friendship seems to be more compelling in developing forms of teaching and learning which connect plausibly with a maximalist form of Islamic education. Firstly, friendship can take the form of mutual attachment—a matter of doing things together—where both Muslim teachers and learners demonstrate a willingness to give priority to one another in terms of time and resources. In other words, when teaching and learning takes place, both teachers and learners avoid being dismissive of one another, that is, they listen with interest and appreciation to one another. In this way, the possibility that they correct one another and learn from the strengths of wisdom of one another in an atmosphere of trust, goodwill and mutual benefit is enhanced (Sherman, 1997: 206–207). When teachers and learners attend to one another with interest and appreciation in an atmosphere of non-dismissiveness, they care for one another in such a way that the potentialities of all the parties are realised. For instance, in such an environment, when learners produce arguments they are not afraid of being corrected by teachers and other learners. They are also not concerned about having their judgementsdismissed by teachers. Such a situation gives rise to critical learning for the reason that teachers attend to and reflect upon learners' judgements with interest and, in turn, learners have to give an account of their reasons, which teachers and fellow learners would invariably take into systematic controversy. In a different way, I find my learners becoming more critical if I become attached to them—that is, if I listen to their views with interest, appreciation and care. For their part, learners expect to be corrected if their reasons cannot be justified. In this way, friendship is nurtured and the possibility of attending to the learners' reasons in an atmosphere of respect and sharing would carry considerable weight.

Secondly, Sherman (1997: 208) argues that friendship entails that people become mutually attuned to one another. In other words, they relax their boundaries and become stimulated by one another through argument. When learners and teachers engage in argumentation on the basis that they relax their boundaries it seems rather unlikely that their deliberations would result in antagonism and conflicts which could potentially thwart their dialogical engagement. However, my potential critic might quite correctly claim that deliberative argumentation favours those learners who are eloquent and that not all learners could defensibly articulate their views. I agree, and for this reason I want to complement Sherman's idea of mutual attunement with Young's (1996) idea of listening to the stories of others, irrespective of whether these narratives are recounted in ways that do not attend to strict rules of argumentation. If Muslim teachers were to do so, the possibility of mutual attunement would further be enhanced. Failing to create spaces for inarticulate, non-eloquent voices would not only exclude legitimate learner voices from learning activities but would also truncate critical learning, which involves openly and fairly evaluating the reasons of others while also showing respect for their points of view no matter how inarticulate they might be. I cannot imagine learners becoming critical if they are prematurely excluded from learning on the grounds that they lack certain levels of articulation.

Thirdly, Sherman's idea of mutual action (1997: 212) occurring among teachers and students is in some ways linked to Arendt's (1998) notion of initiating learners into new ways of doing. This means that when teachers teach, they initiate learners into new understandings and meanings perhaps not thought of before. Similarly, when learners learn, they (de)construct meanings in ways that open up new possibilities for their learning. In this way, teaching and learning is continuous because every initiative taken by teachers and learners is believed to open up possibilities of seeing things anew—that is, meanings are always in the rendering the outcomes of Islamic education as inconclusive. What follows from such a view of teaching and learning is that the outcomes of Islamic education are always incomplete and there always seems to be the possibility that something new will arise. Such a form of mutual action would give much hope for critical learning on the basis that such learning is connected to something new arising.

Sherman's idea of friendship as mutuality would invariably sustain maximalist forms of Islamic education, more specifically teaching and learning, for the reason that such a view of education has in mind that teachers and learners connect with one another, engage deliberatively through argument and narrative, and (de)construct meanings that are always inconclusive. However, such an account of friendship is not sufficient to ensure that teaching and learning remains critical. Why not? Mutual attachment can have the effect that teachers and learners listen to one another with interest and appreciation; mutual attunement can create possibilities for deliberative engagement; and mutual action can ensure that the outcomes of education are inconclusive and the products of new initiatives. Yet, such forms of mutuality are not sufficient to ensure that teaching and learning is ongoing in the sense that new possibilities for sustaining criticality are opened up. For instance, when learners learn to analyse, evaluate and modify arguments and judgements, the possibility exists that they abandon previously held preferences, opinions and views, and explore alternatives, even if it means taking undue risks. Likewise, when teachers teach, they do not restrict their teaching to the achievement of expected or perhaps unexpected outcomes. This would mark the end of education because teachers have not ventured far enough in pursuit of the unintended or the lucky find—that is, they have not taken sufficient risks and have thus limited their explorations. Such a situation would also limit friendship, because friendship cannot last unless teachers have enough confidence in learners—friends—to take risks without knowing in advance what the outcomes might be, that is, without necessarily expecting something positive in return. It is for this reason that I am also attracted to the views of Derrida (1997) who develops a conception of friendship that can positively contribute to addressing some of the limitations of mutuality—in particular encouraging learners to take risks.

I shall now extend the idea of friendship as mutuality to a friendship of 'love' as found in the seminal thoughts of Derrida. Derrida (1997) raises the question of the positive contribution friendship can make in dialogue with others. For him, friendship is the act of loving (*philia*) rather than letting oneself be loved or being loved—what he refers to as inducing love (Derrida, 1997: 8). Of course, it is possible that one can be loved without knowing it. But, it is impossible to love without knowing it. Derrida (1997: 9) makes the claim that 'the friend is the person who loves (and declares his or her love) before being the person who is loved'. And, if one thinks friendship, one is to start with the 'friend-who-loves' not with the 'friend-who-is-loved' (Derrida, 1997: 9). Thus, when Muslim teachers and learners consider themselves to be friends, they willingly declare their love to one another to 'the limit of its possibility' (Derrida, 1997: 12). I feel myself loving my learners when I care for them in a way that evokes their potentialities in order that they come up with possibilities I might not even have thought of. Without being affectionate towards them, I cultivate in them the capacity to reach their own justifiable conclusions to which they are to be held accountable by and to others. Only then can I consider myself as a 'friend-who-loves', since I do not expect being loved in return, that is, when learners reach their own justifiable conclusions about Islamic educational issues, they do so without having to please me—without loving me in return. Similarly, when learners come up with sufficiently good reasons for acting and imagining alternative possibilities so as to be able to re-educate themselves rationally about educational issues without having to please me, they can be said to be 'friends-who-love'. It is this idea of friendship that can go some way towards achieving critical learning.

Why? If I teach students, then I must first declare myself a 'friend-who-loves', since I would not expect to be loved in return. In *The Art of Loving* Fromm (1957: 36) describes such a loving relationship as an attitude, an orientation of character that determines the relatedness of a person to others in the context in which they find themselves. In other words, loving relationships are 'brotherly' (sisterly) because they invoke a sense of responsibility, care and respect towards others (Fromm, 1957: 37). This would imply that as the teacher I should create conditions whereby learners learn authentically, which requires that the following moves be put in place: encouraging learners to imagine situations in and beyond the parameters of their research interests, where things would be better—that is, to be caring towards learners; democratising our interactions whereby learners can take the initiative to imagine possibilities not otherwise thought of—that is, to be responsible towards learners; and connecting with learners' storytelling with the aim of discovering untapped possibilities—that is, to be respectful towards learners. So, a Muslim teacher does not only connect with learners, deliberate with them, and nurture activities in ways where the outcomes are unintended, but also establishes possibilities whereby learners can come up with meanings that they (teachers) might not have expected. In other words, through the teachers' teaching, the possibility exists for learners to come up with defensible meanings irrespective of what their teachers might want. In order for this to happen, learners should be encouraged to take risks (as teachers' friends), because taking risks involves venturing into the unknown and the unexpected—from which unforeseen possibilities might arise. So, teachers who 'love' their learners as friends are desirous for learning to result in unimagined possibilities—ways of doing that teachers had perhaps not thought of before; ways they might not have expected learners to come up with. For instance, when a learner learns, then the unexpected can be expected. That is, he or she is capable of performing what is 'infinitely improbable' (Arendt, 1998: 178). In doing so a learner not only announces what he or she does, has done and intends to do, but also seeks to do the unexpected (Arendt, 1998: 179). One way of ensuring that one acts without knowing what to expect can be to stand back or detach oneself from one's own reasons and ask if others' reasons are in fact justifiable or not. One would not know what to expect if one sets out to evaluate, for instance, what one considers to be master Islamic texts. And when one evaluates these texts (through engaging in systematic controversy with them), one would invariably set out to revise one's own reasons, or abandon them, or replace them with other unexpected reasons (MacIntyre, 1999: 91). In this way one detaches oneself from one's own reasons to revise or abandon them in the light of what others with whom one engages—in this case, the authors of texts—have to say. MacIntyre (1999: 96) argues that we come to know when we are able not just to evaluate our reasons as better or worse, but also when we detach ourselves from the immediacy of our own desires in order to 'imagine alternative realistic futures' which might give rise to unexpected results. This implies that it would be inconceivable to read Islamic texts as master works with which one should not engage and not to stand back from one's rational judgements about one's understandings of these texts. Detaching oneself from one's own reasons in relation to one's evaluation of Islamic texts suggests that these texts cannot be treated *un*critically and *un*controversially. The mere fact that one acts through evaluation and detachment brings into question the underlying assumptions of texts that one reads and analyses. Only then can the unexpected be anticipated, which suggests than only then is one acting—and learning.

In sum, I have argued that critical teaching and learning can best be achieved by means of mutuality and love—more specifically complementary forms of friendship. These forms of friendship have in mind what a maximalist view of Islamic education sets out to achieve: taking risks to cultivate sharing, deliberative engagement and the recognition that others' rights have to be respected—a situation to which future *madāris* can hopefully aspire.

Bibliography

Abdullah, A.S. 1982. *Educational theory: A Quranic outlook*. Makkah: Educational and Psychological Research Center, Umm al-Qurā University.

Ajam, M.T. 1990. Muslim student-teachers and the secular teacher training-programme. In S. Dangor, A.M. Mohammed & Y. Mohamed (eds.). *Perspectives on Islamic education*. Johannesburg: Jet Printers, 89–93.

Al-Alwānī, J. 1994. The ethics of disagreement in Islam. Transl. A.W. Hamid. In A.S. al-Shaikh-Ali (ed.). *Islamic ethics*. Herndon, VA: The International Institute of Islamic Thought, 20–35.

Al-Attas, M.N. 1991. *The concept of education in Islam: A framework for an Islamic philosophy of education*. Kuala Lumpur: The International Institute of Islamic Thought and Civilisation.

───── 1995. Prolegomena to the metaphysics of Islam: An exposition of the fundamental elements of the worldview of Islam. Kuala Lumpur: The International Institute of Islamic Thought and Civilisation.

Al-Burūsiy, I.H. 1913. *Tafsīr Rūh al-Bayān* (Vol 3). Istanbul: Matba Usmaniyyah.

Al-Fanjārī, A.S. 1983. *Al-Hurriyyah al-Siyāsiyyah fi al-Islām*. Kuwait: Dār al-Qalam.

Ali, M. 2005. The rise of the Liberal Islam Network (JIL) in contemporary Indonesia. *American Journal of Islamic Social Sciences* 22(1):1–27.

Ali, M.M. 2007. Liberal Islam: An analysis. *American Journal of Islamic Social Sciences* 24(2):44–70.

Alibasic, A. 1999. The right of political opposition in Islamic history and legal theory: An exploration of an ambivalent heritage. *Al-Shajarah* 4(2):231–296.

Al-Nawawi, I.Y. 1988. *Riyād al-Sālihīn* (Vols 1 & 2). Transl. A.R. Shad. Lahore: Kazi.

Al-Rāghib, al-Isfahāni. N.d. *Al-Mufradāt fi Gharib al-Qurān*. Beirut: Dar al-M`arifah.

Al-Rahīm, M. 1987. The roots of revolution in the Qurān. *Dirāsāt Ifrīqiyyah* 3(1):10–11.

Al-Tabatabā`ī, M.H. 1990. *Al-Mīzān Fī Tafsīr al-Qurān* (Vols 1–7). Transl. S.A. Rizvi. Tehran: Offset Press.

Appiah, K.A. 2006. Cosmopolitanism: Ethics in a world of strangers. London: Penguin.

Arendt, H. 1963. *On revolution*. London: Penguin.

───── 1969. *On violence*. London: Allen Lane, Penguin.

───── 1998. *The human condition*. Second edition. Chicago: University of Chicago Press.

Baderin, M.A. 2007. The evolution of Islamic law of nations and the modern international order: Universal peace through mutuality and cooperation. *American Journal of Islamic Social Sciences* 17(2):57–80.

Bagheri, K. & Khosravi, Z. 2006. The Islamic concept of education reconsidered. *American Journal of Islamic Social Sciences* 23(4):88–102.

Barber, B. 2004. *Strong Democracy: Participatory Politics for a New Age*. Berkeley & Los Angeles: University of California Press.

Bashier, Z. 1978. *The Meccan Crucible*. London: Ithaca Press.

Bauman, Z. 1999. *In search of politics*. Cambridge, MA: Polity Press.

───── 2001a. Community: Seeking safety in an insecure world. Cambridge: Polity Press.

───── 2001b. *The individualized society*. Cambridge: Polity Press.

———— 2003. *Liquid love.* Cambridge: Polity Press.

Benhabib, S. (ed.). 1996. *Democracy and difference: Contesting the boundaries of the political.* Princeton, NJ: Princeton University Press.

Benhabib, S. 2002. *The claims of culture: Equality and diversity in the global era.* Princeton, NJ: Princeton University Press.

———— 2006. The philosophical foundations of cosmopolitan norms. In R. Post (ed.). *Seyla Benhabib: Another cosmopolitanism.* Oxford: Oxford University Press, 33–44.

Berggren, J. 2007. More than the Ummah: Religious and national identity in the Muslim world. *American Journal of Islamic Social Sciences* 24(2):71–93.

Biesta, G. 1998. Say you want a revolution…Suggestions for the impossible future of critical pedagogy. *Educational Theory* 48(1):499–510.

———— 2001. 'Preparing for the incalculable': Deconstruction, justice and the question of education. In G. Biesta & D. Egéa-Kuehne, D. (eds.). *Derrida and education.* New York: Routledge, 32–54.

Bilici, M. 2005. American jihad: Representations of Islam in the United States after 9/11. *American Journal of Islamic Social Sciences* 22(1):50–69.

Bradlow, P.R. & Cairns, M. 1978. *The early Cape Muslims.* Cape Town: A.A. Balkema.

Burik, S. 2009. Opening philosophy to the world: Derrida and education in philosophy. *Educational Theory* 59(3):297–312.

Callan, E. 1997. *Creating citizens: Political education and liberal democracy.* Oxford: Oxford University Press.

———— 1999. A note on patriotism and utopianism: Response to Schrag. *Studies in Philosophy and Education* 18:197–201.

Cavell, S. 1979. *The claim of reason: Wittgenstein, skepticism, morality, and tragedy.* Oxford: Clarendon Press.

Chohan, A.A. 1988. Muslim education in South Africa: Its present position (special emphasis on the Western Cape). *Muslim Education Quarterly* 5(2):67–75.

Christiano, T. 1990. Freedom, consensus, and equality in collective decision making. *Ethics: An International Journal of Social, Political, and Legal Philosophy* 101(1):151–181.

Cilliers, J.L. 1983. Die Tabligh-beweging en sy invloed op die Islam in Suid-Afrika. Unpublished master's thesis, University of the Western Cape, Bellville.

Cowan, J.M. (ed.). 1976. *Hans Wehr: A dictionary of modern written Arabic.* New York: Spoken Language Services.

Crow, K.D. 2000. Nurturing Islamic peace discourse. *American Journal of Islamic Social Sciences* 17(3):54–69.

Da Costa, Y. 1990. Islam in greater Cape Town: A study in the geography of religion. Unpublished doctoral dissertation, University of South Africa, Pretoria.

———— 1992. Assimilatory processes amongst the Cape Muslims in South Africa during the 19th century. *South African Journal of Sociology* 23(1):1–15.

———— 1994a. From social cohesion to religious discord: The life and times of Shaykh Muhammad Salih Hendricks (1871–1945). In Y. da Costa & A. Davids (eds.). *Pages from Cape Muslim history.* Pietermaritzburg: Clyson Printers, 103–114.

—— 1994b. The influence of tasawwuf on Islamic practices at the Cape. In Y. da Costa & A. Davids (eds.). *Pages from Cape Muslim history*. Pietermaritzburg: Clyson Printers, 129–142.

Dangor, S. 1994. In the footsteps of the companions: Shaykh Yusuf of Macassar (1626–1699). In Y. da Costa & A. Davids (eds.). *Pages from Cape Muslim history*. Pietermaritzburg: Clyson Printers, 19–46.

Davids, A. 1980. *The mosques of the Bo-Kaap*. Cape Town: The South African Institute of Arabic and Islamic Research.

Davids, A. 1994a. Alternative education: Tuan Guru and the formation of the Cape Muslim community. In Y. da Costa & A. Davids (eds.). *Pages from Cape Muslim history*. Pietermaritzburg: Clyson Printers, 47–56.

—— 1994b. The origins of the Hanafi-Shafi`i dispute and the impact of Abu Bakr Effendi. In Y. da Costa & A. Davids (eds.). *Pages from Cape Muslim history*. Pietermaritzburg: Clyson Printers, 81–102.

Derrida, J. 1997a. *On cosmopolitanism and forgiveness*. London: Routledge.

—— 1997b. *Politics of friendship*. Transl. G. Collins. London: Verso.

—— 1997c. The Villanova Roundtable: A conversation with Jacques Derrida. In J. Caputo (ed.). *Deconstruction in a nutshell: A conversation with Jacques Derrida*. New York: Fordham University Press, 1–41.

—— 2001. The future of the profession or the unconditional university (thanks to the 'Humanities', what could take place tomorrow). In L. Simmons & H. Worth (eds.). *Derrida Down-under*. Palmerston North: Dunmore Press, 233–247.

—— 2004. *Eyes of the university: Right to philosophy 2*. Transl. J. Plug. Stanford: Stanford University Press.

Dwyer, P. 2004. *Understanding social citizenship: Themes and perspectives for policy and practice*. Bristol: Polity Press.

Emerson, S. 2003. *American jihad: The terrorist living among us*. New York: Free Press.

Fay, B. 1996. *Contemporary philosophy of science*. Oxford: Blackwell.

Feinberg, J. 1972. *Social philosophy*. Englewood Cliffs, NJ: Prentice-Hall.

Freeden, M. 1990. Human rights and welfare: A communitarian view. *Ethics: An International Journal of Social, Political, and Legal Philosophy* 100(1):489–502.

Fromm, E. 1957. *The art of loving*. London: Thorsons.

Garrison, J. 1996. A Deweyan theory of democratic listening. *Educational Theory* 46(4):429–451.

Greene, M. 1995. *Releasing the imagination: Articles on education, the arts and social change*. New York: Jossey-Bass.

Griffiths, A.P. 1965. *Philosophical analysis and education*. London: Routledge and Kegan Paul.

Gutmann, A. 1996. Democratic citizenship. In J. Cohen (ed.). *For love of country: Debating the limits of patriotism*. Boston, MA: Beacon Press, 66–71.

Gutmann, A. & Thompson, D. 1996. *Democracy and disagreement: Why moral conflict cannot be avoided in politics and what can be done about it*. Cambridge, MA: Harvard University Press.

Gutmann, A. 2003. *Identity in democracy*. Princeton, NJ: Princeton University Press.

Gyekye, K. 1997. *Tradition and modernity: Philosophical reflections on the African experience*. New York: Oxford University Press.

Habermas, J. 1996a. *Between facts and norms: Contributions to a discourse theory of law and democracy.* Transl. W. Rheg. Cambridge, MA: MIT Press.

——— 1996b. Three normative models of democracy. In S. Benhabib (ed.). *Democracy and difference: Contesting the boundaries of the political.* Princeton, NJ: Princeton University Press, 21–30.

Halstead. J. 2004. An Islamic concept of education. *Comparative Education* 40(4):517–529.

Haron, M. 1988. Islamic education in South Africa. *Muslim Education Quarterly* 5(2):41–54.

Haverhals, B. 2007. The normative foundations of research-based education: Philosophical notes on the transformation of the modern university idea. *Studies in Philosophy and Education* 26(5):419–432.

Heper, M. 2006. A democratic-conservative government by pious people: The Justice and Development Party in Turkey. In I.M. Abu-Rabi (ed.). *The Blackwell companion to contemporary Islamic thought.* London: Blackwell, 345–361.

Hill, T., Jr. 2000. *Respect, pluralism, and justice.* Oxford: Oxford University Press.

Hobhouse, L. 1922. *The elements of social justice.* London: Allen & Unwin.

Kamali, M.H. 1998. The scope of diversity and juristic disagreement (ikhtilāf) in the Sharī`ah. *Islamic Studies* 37(3):315–337.

Kurdi, A.A. 1984. *The Islamic state: A study based on the Islamic Holy Constitution.* London: Mansell.

Lane, E.W. 1984. *Arabic-English Lexicon* (Vols 1 & 2). Cambridge: Islamic Text Society Trust.

Leiser, G. 1986. Notes on the madras in medieval Islamic society. *The Muslim World* 76:16–23.

Lubbe, G. 1989. The Muslim Judicial Council: A descriptive and analytical investigation. Unpublished doctoral dissertation, University of South Africa, Pretoria.

Macedo, S. 1990. *Liberal virtues: Citizenship, virtue and community.* Oxford: Oxford University Press.

MacIntyre, A. 1990. *Three rival versions of modern enquiry: Encyclopaedia, genealogy, and tradition.* London: Duckworth.

——— 1999. *Dependent rational animals: Why human beings need the virtues.* Illinois, Peru: Open Court.

MacIntyre, A. & Dunn, J. 2002. Alasdair MacIntyre in dialogue with Joseph Dunn. *Journal of Philosophy of Education* 36(1):1–19.

Mahida, E.M. 1993. *History of Muslims in South Africa: A chronology.* Durban: Kat Bros. Printers.

Makdisi, G. 1981. *The rise of colleges: Institutions of learning in Islam and the West.* Edinburgh: Edinburgh University Press.

——— 1990. The rise of humanism in classical Islam and the West. Edinburgh: Edinburgh University Press.

Malik, J. 2006. Madrasah in South Asia. In I.M. Abu-Rabi (ed.). *The Blackwell companion to contemporary Islamic thought.* London: Blackwell, 105–121.

McLaughlin, T. 1992. Citizenship, diversity and education: A philosophical perspective. *Journal of Moral Education,* 21(3):235–250.

Merry, M. & De Ruyter, D. 2009. Cosmopolitanism and the deeply religious. *Journal of Beliefs and Values* 30(1):49–60.

Miller, D. 2004. Justice, democracy and public goods. In K. Dowding, R. Goodin & C. Pateman (eds.). *Justice and democracy.* Cambridge: Cambridge University Press, 127–149.

Moosa, E. 1989. Muslim conservatism in South Africa. *Journal of Theology for Southern Africa* 6(1):73–81.

Nadvi, S.H.H. 1988. A critical overview of Muslim education in South Africa. *Muslim Education Quarterly* 5(2):55–66.

Naude, J.A. 1982. The ulama in South Africa with special reference to Transvaal ulama. *Journal for Islamic Studies* 2(1):23–39.

Nāyif, A. 1999. The hieracrchy of the perfect man. *Al-Shajarah* 4(2):175–198.

Nussbaum, M. 1997. *Cultivating humanity: A classical defence of reform in liberal education.* Cambridge, MA: Harvard University Press.

―――― 2001. *Upheavals of thought: The intelligence of emotions.* Cambridge: Cambridge University Press.

Osman, M.F. 2006. Islam, terrorism, and the Western misapprehensions. In I.M. Abu-Rabi (ed.). *The Blackwell companion to contemporary Islamic thought.* London: Blackwell, 377–386.

Pacaci, M. & Aktay, Y. 2006. 75 years of higher religious education in modern Turkey. In I.M. Abu-Rabi (ed.). *The Blackwell companion to contemporary Islamic thought.* London: Blackwell, 122–144.

Papastephanou, M. 2002. Arrows not yet fired: Cultivating cosmopolitanism through education. *Journal of Philosophy of Education* 36(1):69–86.

Phillion, J. 2002. Becoming a narrative inquirer in a multicultural landscape. *Journal of Curriculum Studies* 34(5):535–556.

Popper, K. 1962. *The open society and its enemies: The high tide of prophecy—Hegel, Marx and the aftermath.* London: Routledge & Kegan Paul.

―――― 1989. *Conjectures and refutations: The growth of scientific knowledge.* London: Routledge.

Quin, M. 2010. 'Ex and the city': On cosmopolitanism, community and the 'curriculum of refuge'. *Transnational Curriculum Inquiry* (Forthcoming).

Rahman, F. 1982. *Islam and modernity.* Chicago: Chicago University Press.

―――― 1986. The principle of shura and the role of the ummah in Islam. In M. Ahmad (ed.). *State politics in Islam.* Chicago: American Trust Publications, 91–96.

Rawls, J. 1971. *A theory of justice.* Cambridge, MA: Harvard University Press.

―――― 1993. *Political liberalism.* New York: Columbia Press University.

Rehman, N. 1988. An investigation into the planning and implementation of a madressa teachers diploma for in-service Muslim teachers and adults in the Durban and district areas by the Education Committee of the Muslim Charitable Foundation during 1984–1987. Unpublished MEd thesis, University of South Africa, Pretoria.

Rorty, R. 1988. *Education without dogma.* Dissent, 36(2):198–204.

―――― 1999. *Philosophy and social hope.* London: Penguin.

Ryle, G. 1949. *The concept of mind.* Aylesbury: Hazell Watson and Viney.

Sāfi, L.M. 1988. War and peace. *American Journal of Islamic Social Sciences* 5(1):29–57.

Sahin, B. 2007. Toleration, political liberalism, and peaceful co-existence. *American Journal of Islamic Social Sciences* 24(1):1–24.

Shalaby, A. 1954. *History of Muslim education.* Beirut: Dar AI-Kashshaf.

Sherman, N. 1997. *Making a necessity of virtue: Aristotle and Kant on virtue.* Cambridge: Cambridge University Press.

Siddiqui, O. 2001. Relativism vs. universalism: Islam and the human rights debate. *American Journal of Islamic Social Sciences* 18(1):59–94.

Tahhān, M.M. 1997. *Tahaddiyāt Siyāsiyyah Tuwājih al-Harakah al-Islamiyyah.* Kuwait: Al-Markaz al-Ā`lamī li al-Kitāb al-Islāmi, 63–66.

Tayob, A. 1995. *Islamic resurgence in South Africa: The Muslim Youth Movement.* Cape Town: University of Cape Town Press.

Tibawi, A.L. 1976. *Arabic and Islamic themes: Historical, educational and literary studies.* London: Luzac.

Waghid, Y. 1994. Conceptually based problems within madrassah education in South Africa. *Muslim Education Quarterly* 11(2):9–28.

————— 2009. Education and madrassahs in South Africa: On the possibility of preventing extremism. *British Journal of Religious Education* 31(2):117–128.

Waldron, J. 2006. Cosmopolitan norms. In R. Post (ed.). *Seyla Benhabib: Another cosmopolitanism.* Oxford: Oxford University Press, 83–101.

Walzer, M. 1983. *Spheres of justice: A defense of pluralism and equality.* New York: Basic Books.

Wan Daud, W.M.N. 1990. *The concept of knowledge in Islam and its implications for education in a developing country.* London: Mansell.

Yousif, A.F. 2006. Contemporary Islamic movements in Southeast Asia. In I.M. Abu-Rabi (ed.). *The Blackwell companion to contemporary Islamic thought.* London: Blackwell, 449–465.

Zembylas, M. 2005. A pedagogy of unknowing: Witnessing unknowability in teaching and learning. *Studies in Philosophy and Education* 24(2):137–160.

GLOBAL
STUDIES IN
EDUCATION

A.C. (Tina) Besley, Michael A. Peters,
Cameron McCarthy, Fazal Rizvi
General Editors

Global Studies in Education is a book series that addresses the implications of the powerful dynamics associated with globalization for re-conceptualizing educational theory, policy and practice. The general orientation of the series is interdisciplinary. It welcomes conceptual, empirical and critical studies that explore the dynamics of the rapidly changing global processes, connectivities and imagination, and how these are reshaping issues of knowledge creation and management and economic and political institutions, leading to new social identities and cultural formations associated with education.

We are particularly interested in manuscripts that offer: a) new theoretical, and methodological, approaches to the study of globalization and its impact on education; b) ethnographic case studies or textual/discourse based analyses that examine the cultural identity experiences of youth and educators inside and outside of educational institutions; c) studies of education policy processes that address the impact and operation of global agencies and networks; d) analyses of the nature and scope of transnational flows of capital, people and ideas and how these are affecting educational processes; e) studies of shifts in knowledge and media formations, and how these point to new conceptions of educational processes; f) exploration of global economic, social and educational inequalities and social movements promoting ethical renewal.

For additional information about this series or for the submission of manuscripts, please contact one of the series editors:

A.C. (Tina) Besley: tbesley@illinois.edu   Department of Educational Policy Studies
Cameron McCarthy: cmccart1@illinois.edu   University of Illinois at Urbana-Champaign
Michael A. Peters: mpet001@illinois.edu   1310 South Sixth Street
Fazal Rizvi: frizvi@unimelb.edu.au   Champaign, IL 61820   USA

To order other books in this series, please contact our Customer Service Department:

(800) 770-LANG (within the U.S.)
(212) 647-7706 (outside the U.S.)
(212) 647-7707 FAX

Or browse online by series:
www.peterlang.com